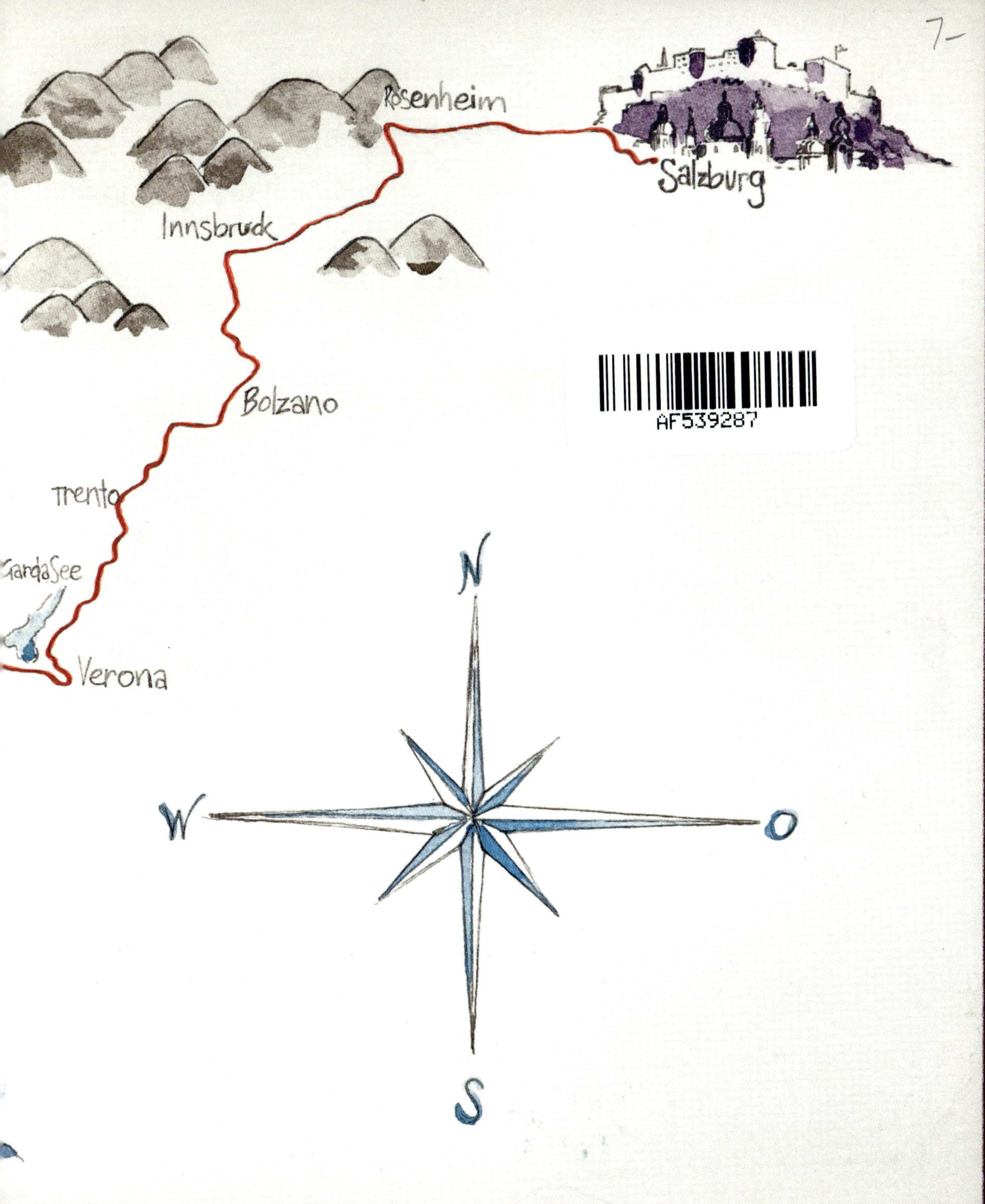
Rosenheim
Salzburg
Innsbruck
Bolzano
Trento
GardaSee
Verona
N
W
O
S

TRAVELS WITH a PORSCHE

Peter Daniell Porsche

For the employees of Porsche Firms,
all Porsche enthusiasts, photographers, offroad-drivers and friends of poetry!

Polzer Publishing

First published April 2010
15,000 copies

Polzer Publishing
Franz Hinterholzer-Kai 22
A-5020 Salzburg
Phone: +43 (0) 662 455 300
kulturverlag@polzer.net
www.polzer.net

ISBN 978-3-902658-19-7

Peter Daniell Porsche: evocative texts, aphorisms, and poems
Tobias Hitsch and Hannes Reithmayr: photos
Manfred Kiwek: design of inside covers
Gail Polacsek: translation from German to English

Printing: Niederösterreichisches Pressehaus, www.np-druck.at
Bookbinding: G.G. Buchbinderei Gesellschaft m.b.H.

TRAVELS WITH a PORSCHE

Peter Daniell Porsche

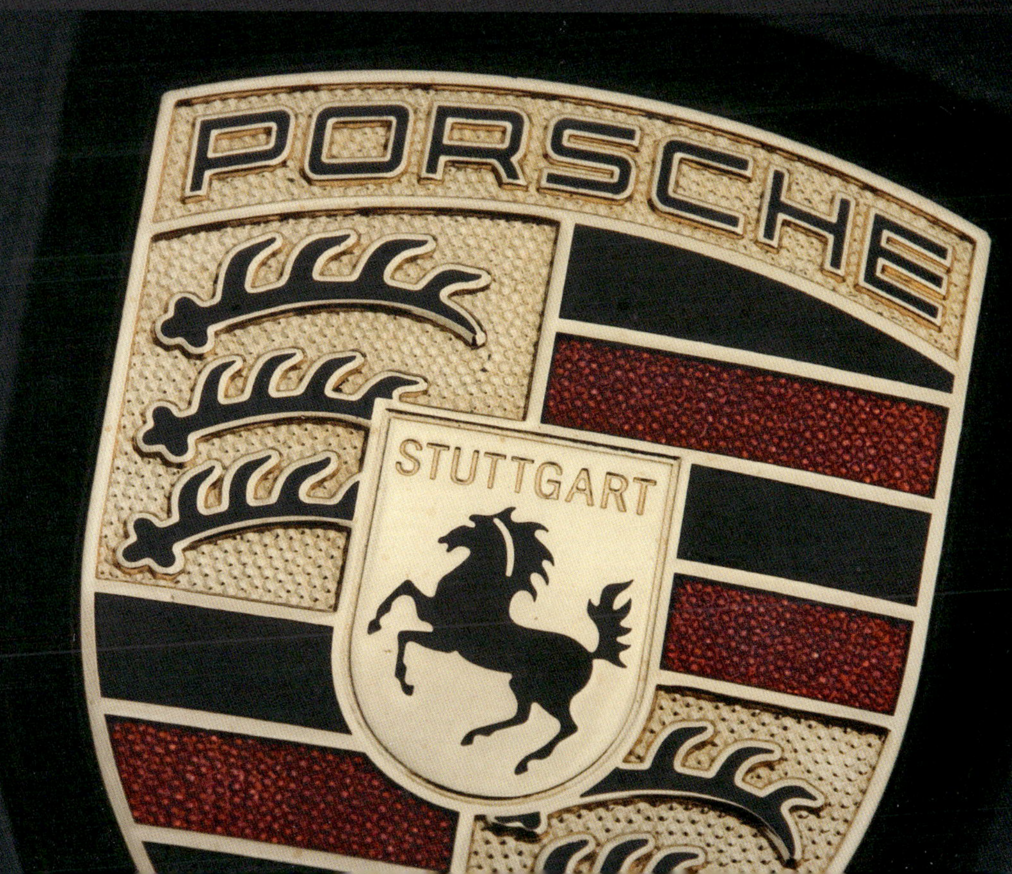

A few introductory words

A journey over the Ligurian Ridge Road with altogether 16 Porsche Cayenne cars gave rise to the creation of this book. At the same time, this particular journey prompted me to turn my mind to many other roads travelled.

Historically
The fact that this Ligurian High Alpine Road between Italy and France was built for the Third Reich, serving, as I see it, to advance the purposes of a dark period of history, is something that should not be ignored, much less forgotten indeed, if acknowledged, it might point to a way of learning from the resulting mistakes and their consequences and thus lead to future growth.

The present issue
We travelled from Salzburg by way of Rosenheim, Innsbruck, the Brenner, Bozen, the Italian Lowlands, Verona, Piacenza, Alessàndria, Torino, Cuneo, Limone Piemonte, the Ligurian High Alpine Road to San Remo with a view to really getting to know and enjoy the Porsche Cayenne under varying conditions.

Team spirit
It was a wonderful and valuable experience to gather people from such different walks of life together, all united by the joys of travel and sharing the same goal.

The story of a family
A brief outline of the Porsche family which today, I am glad to report, can be traced back to the beginning of the 17th century.

A contribution
The sale of this book will, I hope, help to refund what I advanced in support of certain artistic and social projects and to secure their continued existence in the future.

The artistic aspect
Atmospheric sketches, aphorisms and poems from my entire creative work to date, as well as from various already published books are gathered in this volume. Indirectly and on another level, a journey through the year, the course of the day and, indeed, through over half my lifetime is described with the juxtaposing of accompanying poems and photos.

The business aspect

Moreorless unintentionally, this book is coming out at a time when great upheavals are taking place in all sorts of economic areas. The impact on our Porsche companies too is not negligible. Let us hope that the decisions that have been made turn out for the best for all concerned. Let us hope too, that the overall situation in our world may in time develop in such a way that people can show more regard for each other, above all in little things. Only with mutual understanding, after all, can we pave the way for a socially acceptable future. As to the outcome of the future structuring of our firm and the changes this implies, let each of us form our own views!

Indeed, in this context it is not for nothing that the book in hand is called "Travels with a Porsche".

Porsche Travels

Porsche Jacobus, circa 1600, occupation unknown
Porsche Christophorus, circa 1630, occupation unknown
Porsche Johann, 1671, farmer
Porsche Gottfried, 1705, clothworker
Porsche Johann Joseph, 1726, farmer
Porsche Johannes Wenzel Aloisius, 1753, tabellarius, official courier
Porsche Anton(ius), 1778, house owner, pipe constructor in gentleman's employ
Porsche Ferdinand, 1820, dressmaker, house owner, master tailor, smith
Porsche Anton, 1845, plumber, house owner, master panel-beater
Porsche Eng. D. (hon.) Ferdinand, 1875, Professor and motor-vehicle designer
Porsche Ferdinand (Ferry) Anton Ernst, 1909, engineer, manufacturer
Porsche Hans-Peter, 1940, engineer
Porsche Peter Daniell, 1973, music therapist, Waldorf teacher, freelance poet

Peter Daniell Porsche

I was born in 1973 in Stuttgart. Music therapist, Waldorf teacher and freelance poet, I grew up in Salzburg, where I attended the Salzburg Waldorf Kindergarten and the Rudolf Steiner School through to the 12th grade. Early love of plants and animals thanks to the example and opportunities provided by my mother. My awareness of money and economic subjects came initially from my father. I took a great interest in technical and new developments both intellectually and in practice. Early lessons in piano playing, violin, recorder, and flute – the latter remaining my main instrument. Move to Stuttgart, my place of birth, to attend the Uhlandshöhe Waldorf-School where I graduated with a high-school diploma. Embarked upon Waldorf education studies in Dornach in Switzerland. Returned to Salzburg to spend 14 months serving with the Austrian Red Cross, which afforded me many very special impressions and memorable experiences. Study of anthroposophy-oriented music therapy in Berlin (Havelhöhe).

Trainee-ship as music therapist in Munich (Friedel-Eder-School) and Stuttgart (Filderklinik). Conclusion of the recognized teacher training and music therapy training in the Paracelsus-School in Salzburg (educational institute for children and young people lacking emotional and social skills). I then took over the chairmanship of the Paracelsus-School-Association and the building of the new school premises in St. Jakob am Thurn near Puch. This led to the foundation of the Cultural Centre of St. Jakob with the Paracelsus School, the Jakob's Hall and the organic restaurant, Schützenwirt. I have been continually active as developer and site-manager and as advisor and support in the development of numerous other social, educational and artistic projects.
Porsche Cayenne driver, Porsche tractor driver and Porsche hot-air balloon flyer! I am married and father of three children – for which heartfelt thanks!

My Thanks

At this point I would like to thank my dear wife for her constant support and the generosity she showed in many ways behind the scenes. Without her my work and activities up to now, including this book, would, to a great extent, not have been possible. My thanks to my friend Stefan who originally guided me to the way over the Ligurian High Alpine Road. I would also like to thank the entire staff of the Cultural Centre in St. Jakob for sorting out the inordinate amount of red-tape necessary over the period of more than two years prior to the journey, as well as the finishing touches afterwards.
Thank you to the photographer, Tobias Hitsch, for most of the photos and the lay-out of this book and to Hannes Reithmayr too, for the few but very special photos and his energetic co-organisation of the journey beforehand and afterwards.
My thanks to Evelyne Bauer and Birgit Ertl in my office for attending to so many aspects of this project, to Gail Polacsek for her translation and to Julian Nüesch for the accompanying film (www.einporschegehtaufreisen.at).
I thank the publishers and especially Bodo Polzer for the realization of the book and the proof-readers, typesetters, printers and bookbinders for its completion. As well, thank-you to the retailers and all those who co-operated in the marketing, in the keen distribution and sales of the book!
I am thankful that this journey could be carried through without any serious hitches, accidents or damages and that the weather was kind enough to offer us for those two days the right sort of setting for our venture. And so this expedition became a dream come true.

A living legend

The Porsche legend lives on no matter how times may change, because, once brought to life in our hearts and minds, it is everlasting.
The story tells of luck, favour, hard work, courage, success, tradition and innovation – a story

about elegance and love of detail, beauty of form, unpretentiousness and reserve. But there is sacrifice and defeat as well, and then insight and starting afresh. And so it is hardly surprising that the true Porsche enthusiasts, knowing how favoured they are, would never boast. They are decent, polite and ready to help, open, loyal and true. To be among Porsche enthusiasts is to be among kindred spirits, as in a big family. When two Porsche drivers pass on the road they usually greet each other with the sign meaning "excellent" made by forming a ring with the tips of the thumb and the index finger of the right hand. This is what my great-grandfather used to do at races to spur on his racing-driver when the Porsche was out ahead of the others! May this favour and tradition live on in the Porsche saga and may new Porsche enthusiasts discover it anew, whatever the future.

Whatever the future

It is born of the present and rooted in the past. Looking at the chronicles of our family, one sees that all our ancestors whose occupation is known were either upright craftsmen or clear thinkers. Although unfortunately I never knew my great-grandfather, Dr. Ferdinand Porsche personally, I nonetheless see him as the thinker and craftsman combined in one person. The rigorous genius with the cool head, the capable hands and the future always in his sights! With this in mind I am above all deeply grateful to my great-grandfather for his life work which, with the toil of his own hands too, was founded for the future. However, this world being what it is, no sooner does a man address a task, than the forces of both good and evil come into play. No human act can be maintained with the impetus of the initial intention for good, and work out uniquely for the good. Every action draws with it unintentional changes.
No doubt my great-grandfather was not perfect either but he strove unremittingly for the future good, and not merely for himself. In truth, we human beings are not inherently bad but by the very fact of being human, we are the recipients of freedom for good and for evil; we bear the freedom of our physical upright stature, the capacity to think and the power to use our own freedom of choice. It is therefore incumbent upon us in acknowledging evil for what it is, to recognize the good and to make it our endeavour as human beings to reach out for the good ever more ardently.

With this in mind I wish to quote certain words of Dr. Rudolf Steiner, with whom my grandmother had the honour of being personally acquainted, and which are very close to my heart. May the wisdom of these words sustain us all in the best possible way:

"For in future times human beings will have to be each for each and not one through another. Thus the world's destiny will be reached, when each one rests within himself and each gives to each that which no one chooses to claim."

What no one chooses to claim

A lofty and sublime ideal – and please do not imagine that I might be able to attain it as a rule – not at all! But it remains nevertheless my endeavour. And this book too may be considered an attempt to find a new way of looking at such diverse subjects as art and technology, nature and industry, social principles and material joint ventures and despite their inherent contrasts, bring them together.

It is simply a book with a difference – Porsche is in many ways the main focus but facts and figures purposely do not feature here. There is no page numbering: it is purely for leafing through, a book for the eye, the ear, the heart and the head. Not a normal-sized book of photography – no, rather small and inconspicuous – quite of a size for carrying about with you. It is meant as a book for Porsche enthusiasts, for poets, artists, photographers, the outdoor type, engineers… for rich and poor, young and old… May this book succeed in forging many links in the best possible way.

Linking up

This book aims to compare two distinct and separate planes: with the photographs it addresses technology, with the poems, the spiritual-divine world. The reader-observer is thus placed ever-active in the middle of both worlds – a situation which confronts us constantly in our daily life and which it becomes increasingly urgent for us to recognize.

An attempt to link thinking, feeling and willing with social work, teaching and therapy, art and culture as well as science and finance.

May this intention, in principle at least, succeed!

Hoping that you enjoy leafing through this book, reflecting and sharing.

Yours,

Peter Daniell Porsche
Zistelalpe, 23. July 2009

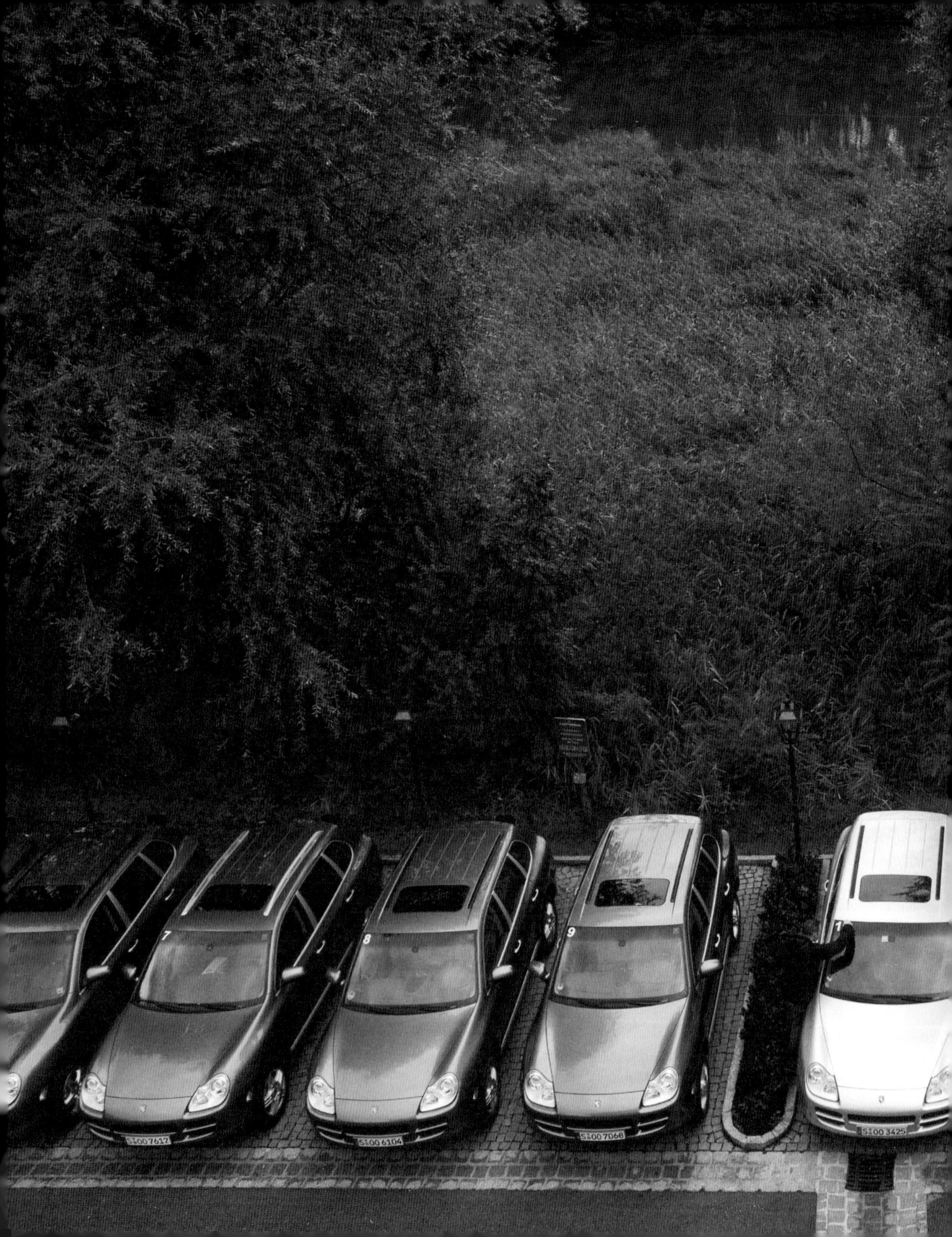
7
8
9
1
S 00 7617
S 00 6104
S 00 7068
S 00 3425

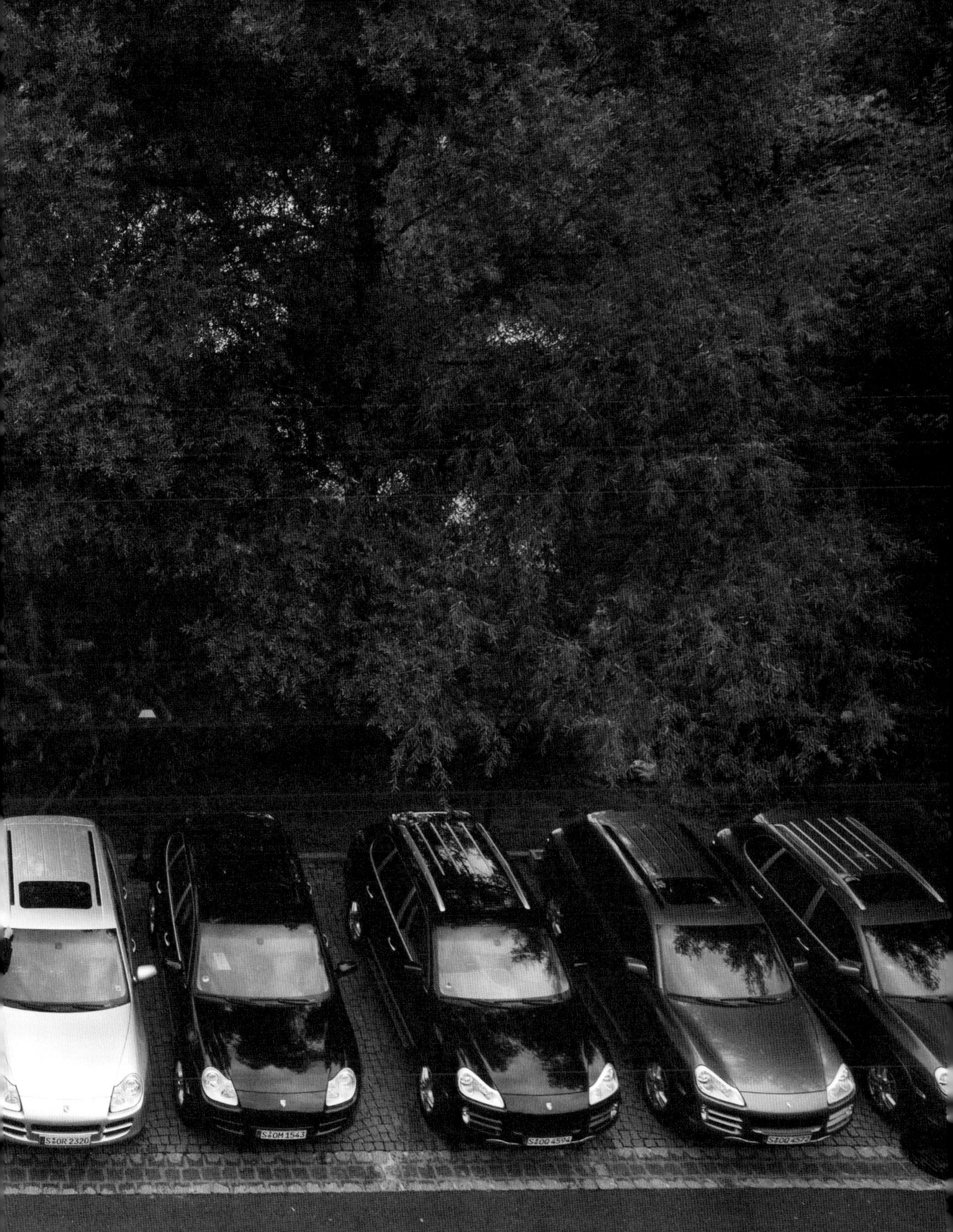
S OR 2320
S OM 1543

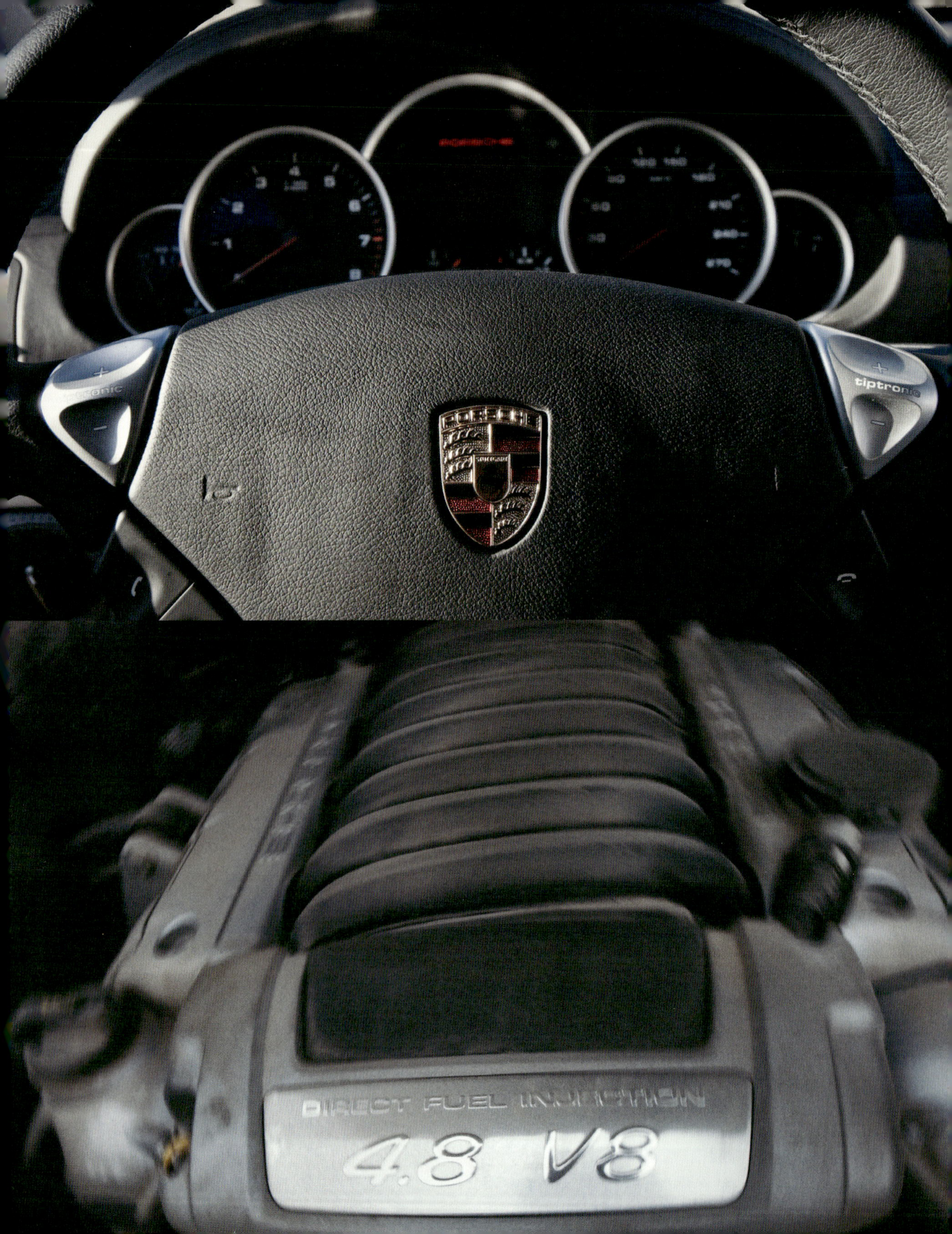
PORSCHE
tiptronic
DIRECT FUEL INJECTION
4.8 V8

Creation

There was once upon a time, aeons long ago,
Remote in a far-away twilight land,
A primeval stream unstirred by human hand;
Veering constellations spun their dim glow
Earth and space turbulent with cyclones from the sea –
Later oracles their dark reflections show –
Spheres of light gyrating, deliberate, slow.

Waves of luminous beings now wafted gently
In the realm between substance and spirit;
They were nurtured withal by the life of yon stream…
Hereafter in blue morning ascending soft

A sun-sphere rose day for day aloft,

Pouring its rays on waters, field and fen
On stone, plants and creatures created then –
Resplendent vitality showing, and yet,
Sufficing alone not for the making of men –
Creation He breathed upon the human being.
Henceforth life went on growing and dying away –
Ever striving, steadfast day after day.

In The Morning Light

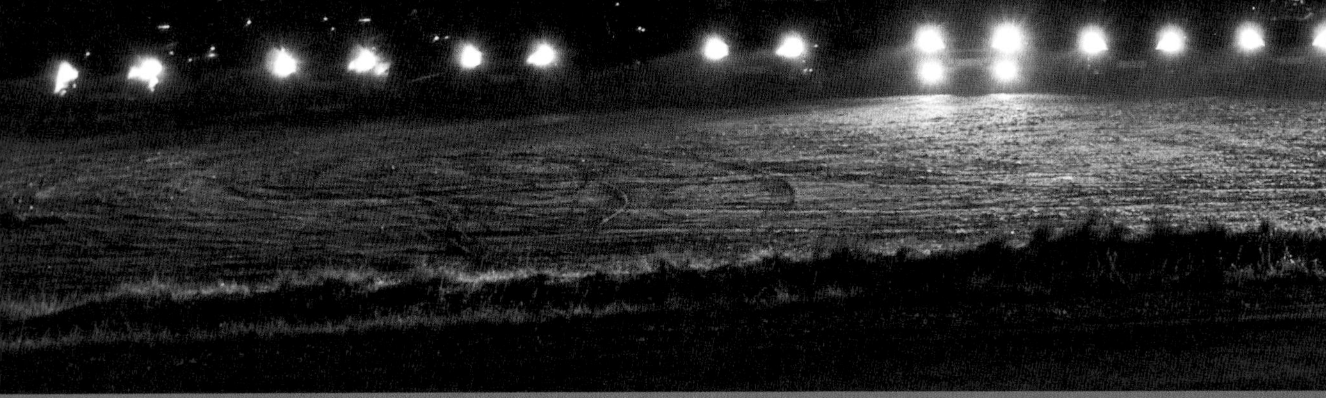

The moon lingers still in the firmament
And stars glister through from the deep of night
Becalmed lies the world in enchanted glow
Till softly shimmering arches the blue
To reach a surmise of the mountain's crest
And arouse the animal world from sleep.
As the first bird sound rings out from the bough
All-pervasive unfolds this new today
From the mists of time for infinity,
At this moment the here and now to greet.

Cold stirs the air in the woods and meadows
Yet presently hope comes filtering through

As if for the first time, wonderfully,
Soft clouds mass in the celestial blue.

In peach-blossom tones bright with ruddy gleam
The sun breaks the spell with its morning shafts
Casting heaven's light o'er the festive hour
So that rocks, the plants, the beasts and man
In the radiant warmth of that ball of fire
O'er the horizon ascending now,
May each in their own way rejoice in the light –
And as we go forth to our needful tasks
May the morning light see us start aright
And accompany us all the days of our life!

You will learn to be silent
when you long for speech.

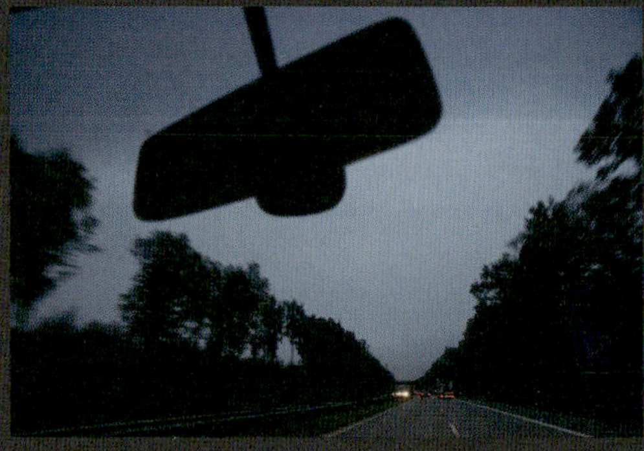

Though everything seems measurable,
thought remains beyond measure.

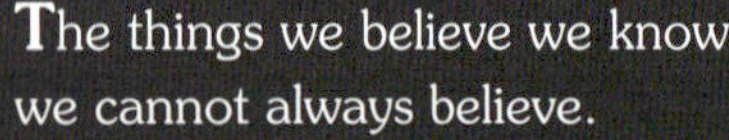

The things we believe we know
we cannot always believe.

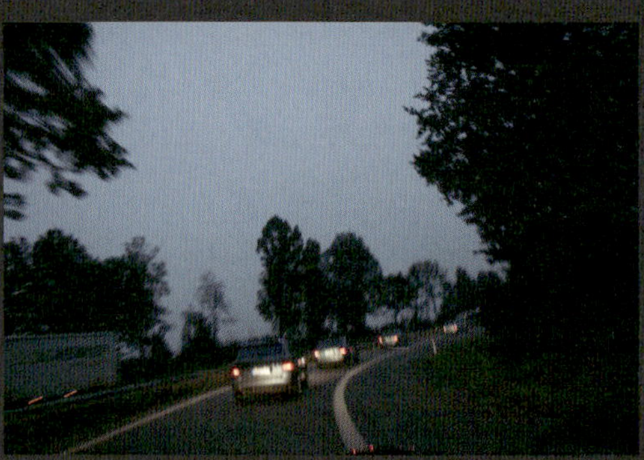

How little we learn of feelings
to which we are a stranger.

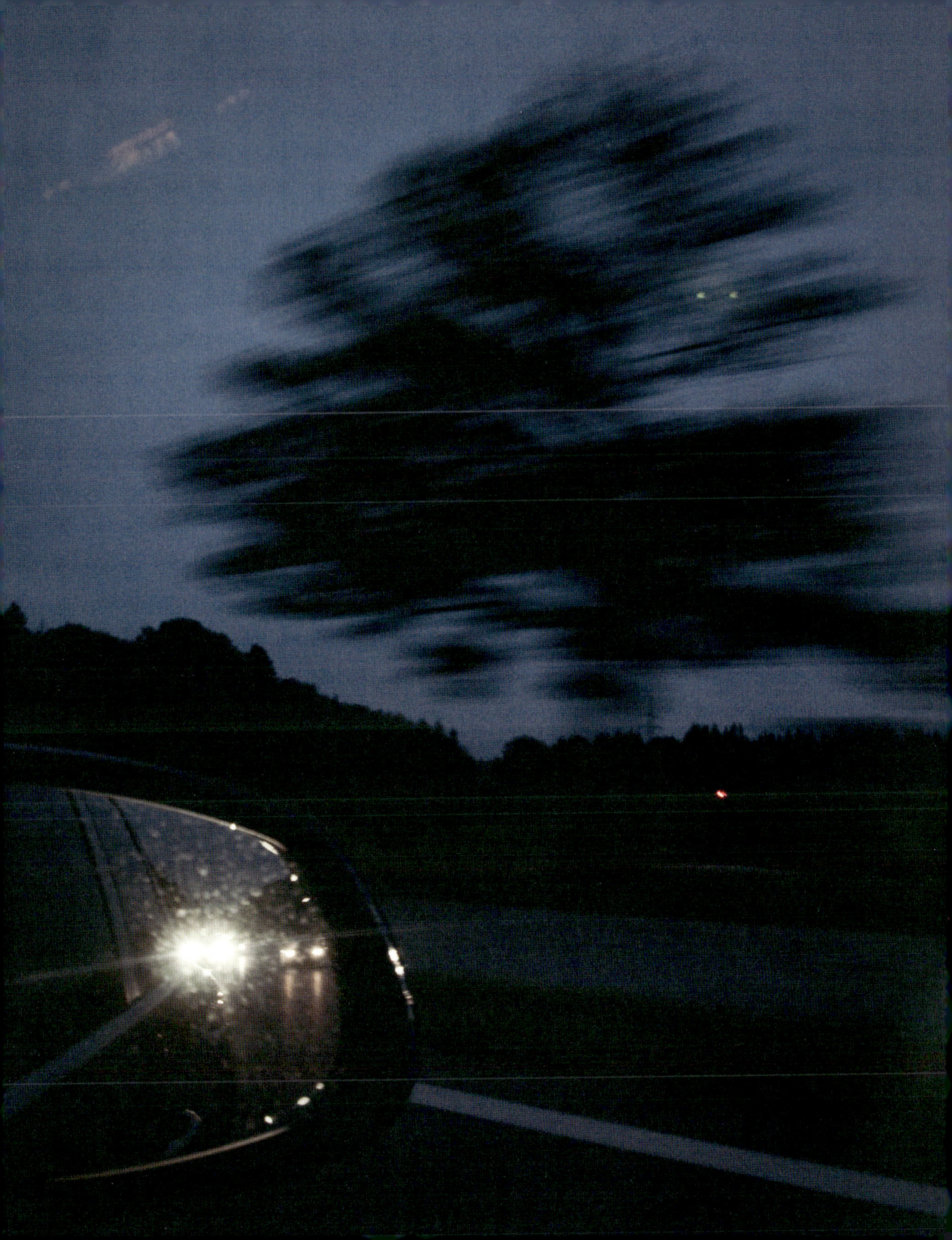

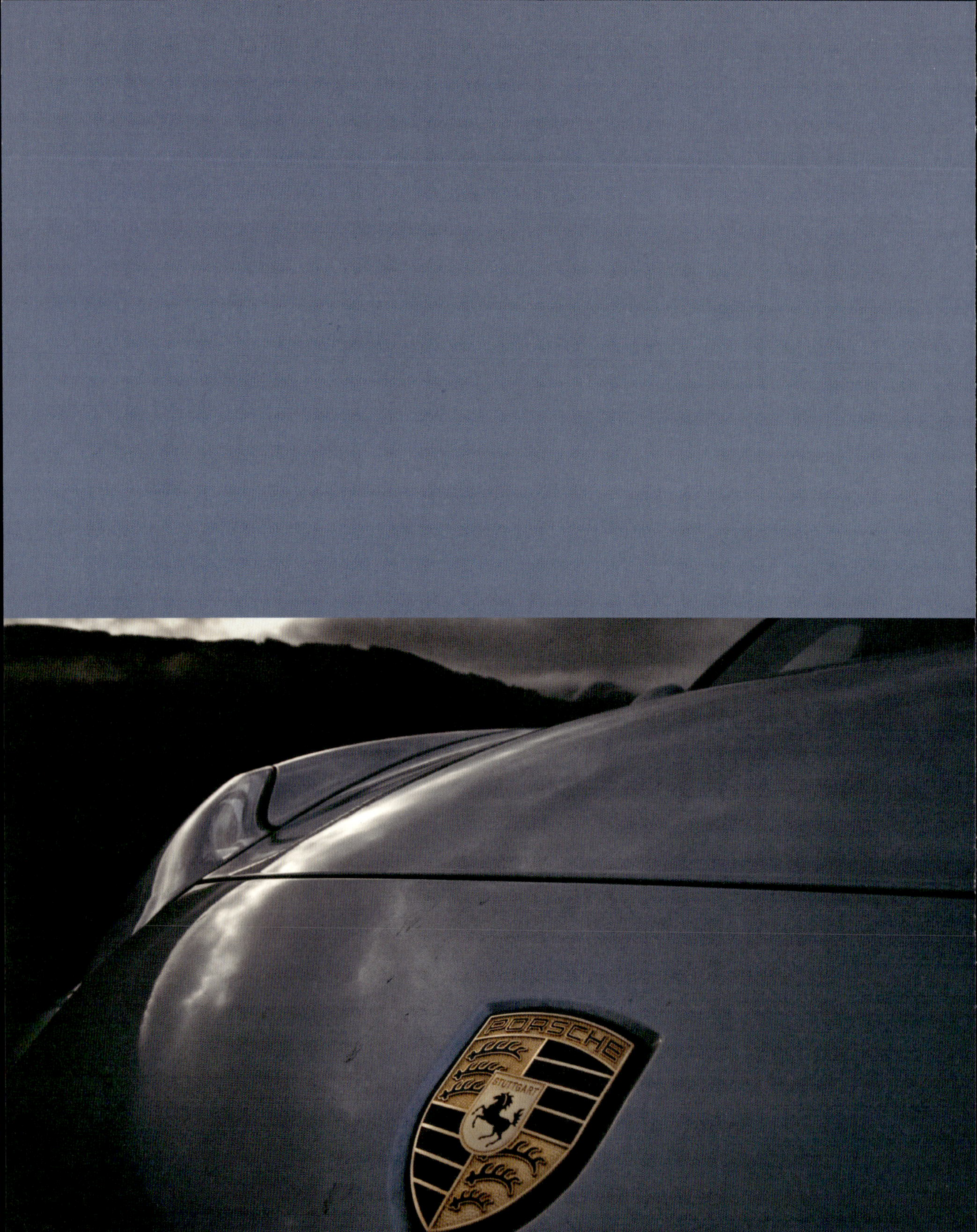
PORSCHE
STUTTGART

Distance

Space streams on and on –
all sound ceases…
the universe shines eternally –

But soon, tho' not as soon
as a dream loses its reality…

Two days in time swift race…
space streams on and on –
onward to eternity…

To The New Year

A New Year just as came round last year,
Brings a new chance kindliness to maintain –
Friend, its not so easy to be humane
But the time for resolutions is here.

A new day all brightness pure and clear,
Will show the way new objectives to gain,
Friend, in true love our faith we retain,
There's no sense of pain yet in this New Year.

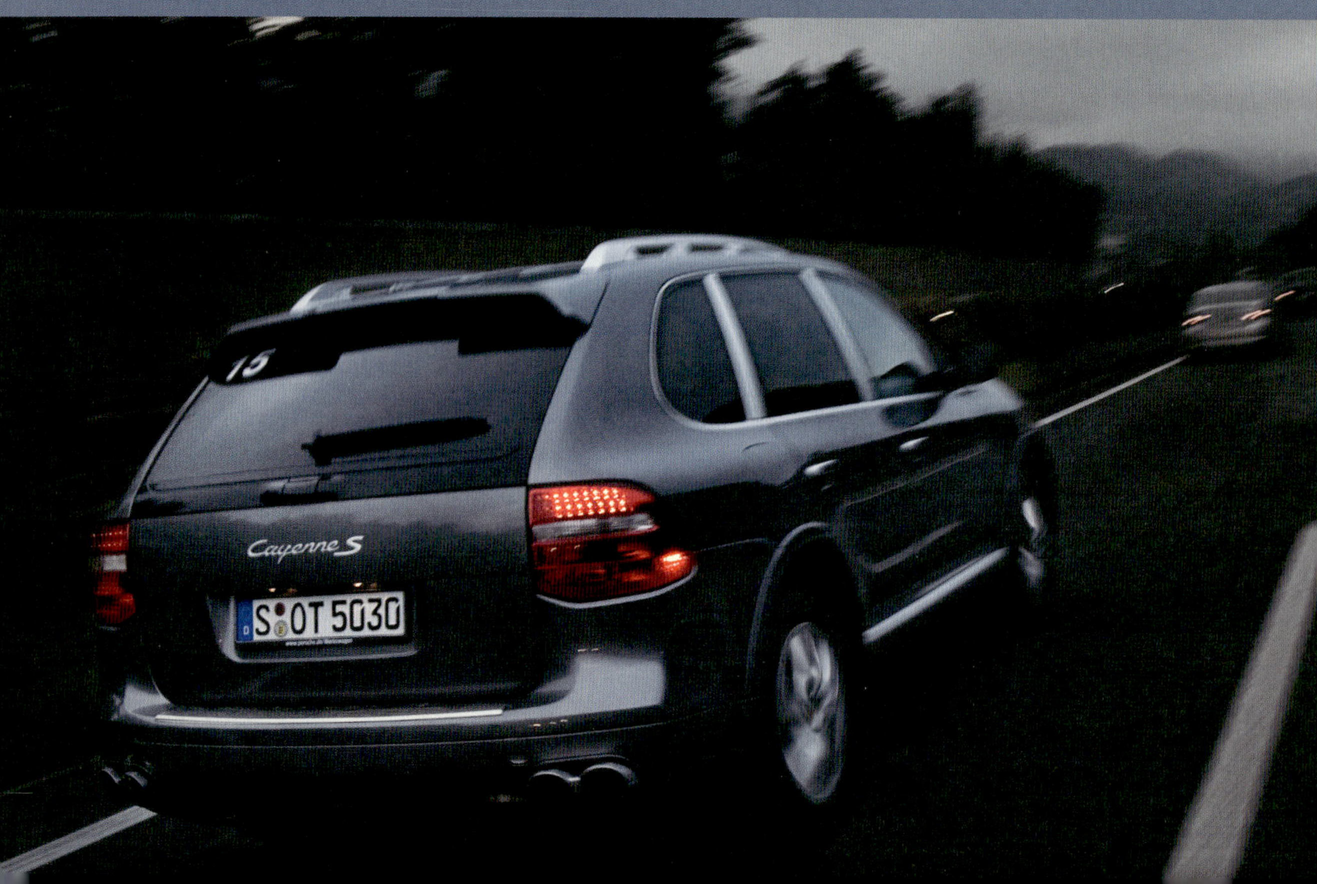

And if the day dawns when again and again
The year brings its weight of sorrow and pain
It will not do, to always complain.

A person with true regard for mankind
Will never life's mysteries disdain
But embrace what is and the still undefined.

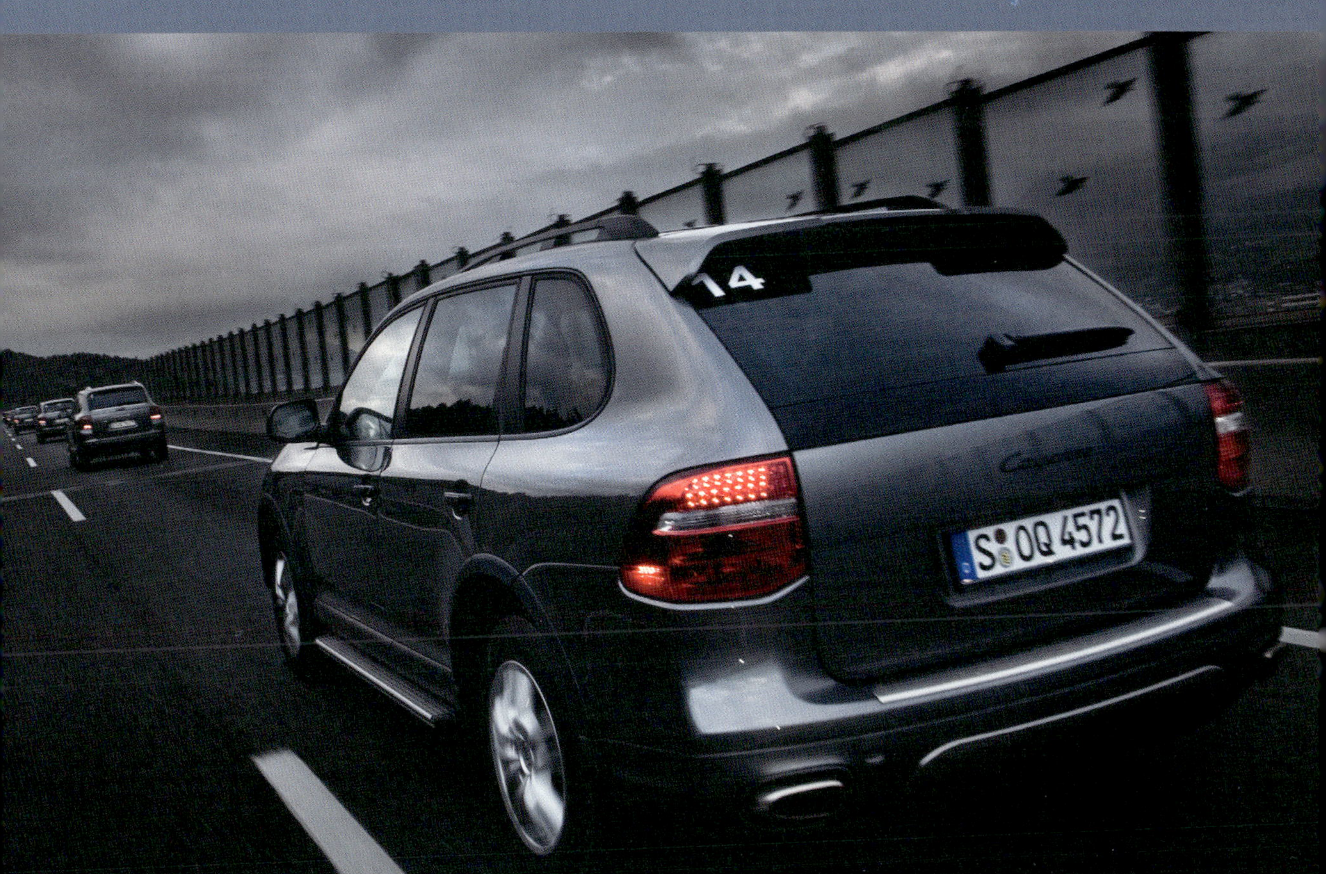

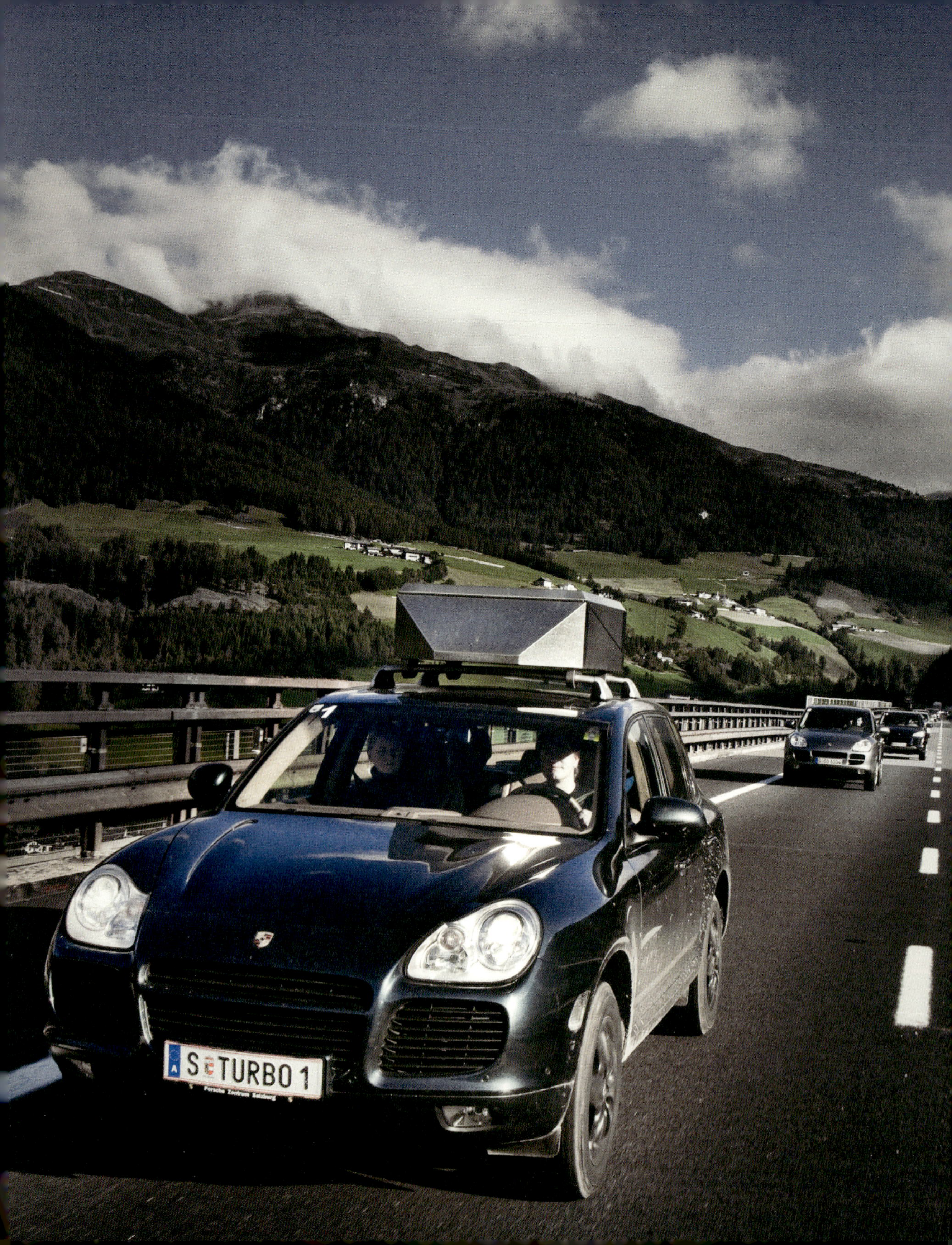
S TURBO 1

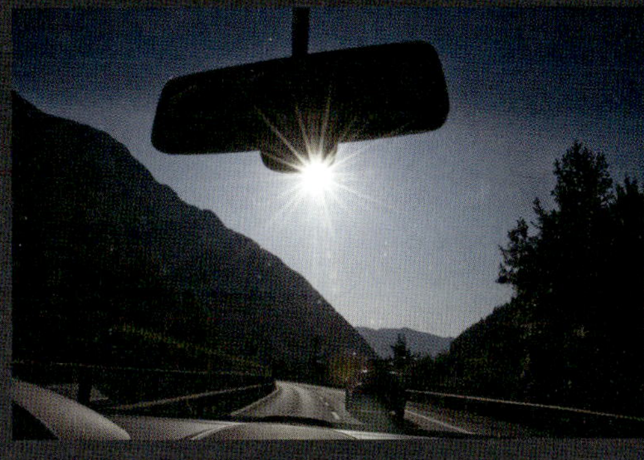

A fleeting glance says a lot
but a good look
has something more to say.

Even though it takes a long time
to reach one's goal
it is still always
only the beginning.

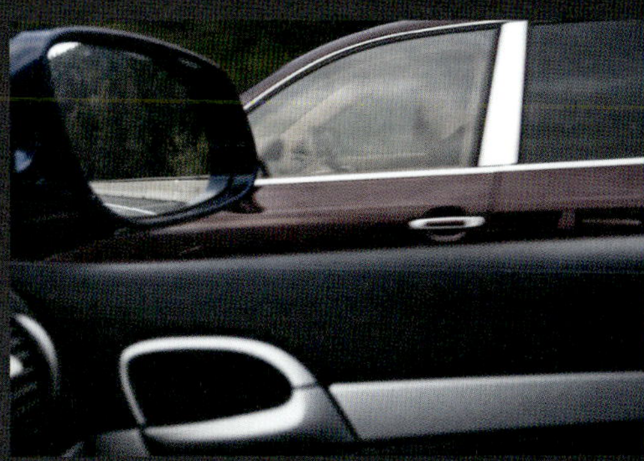

Not until one has learnt abstention
can one appreciate
not having to abstain.

We have forgotten
how to see unthinkingly,
we must learn to understand with our eyes.

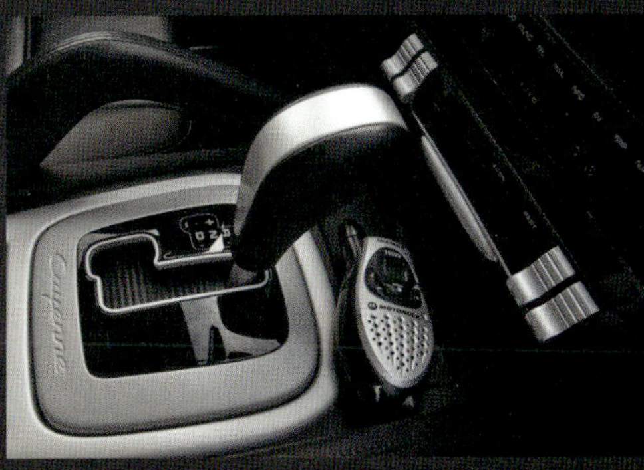

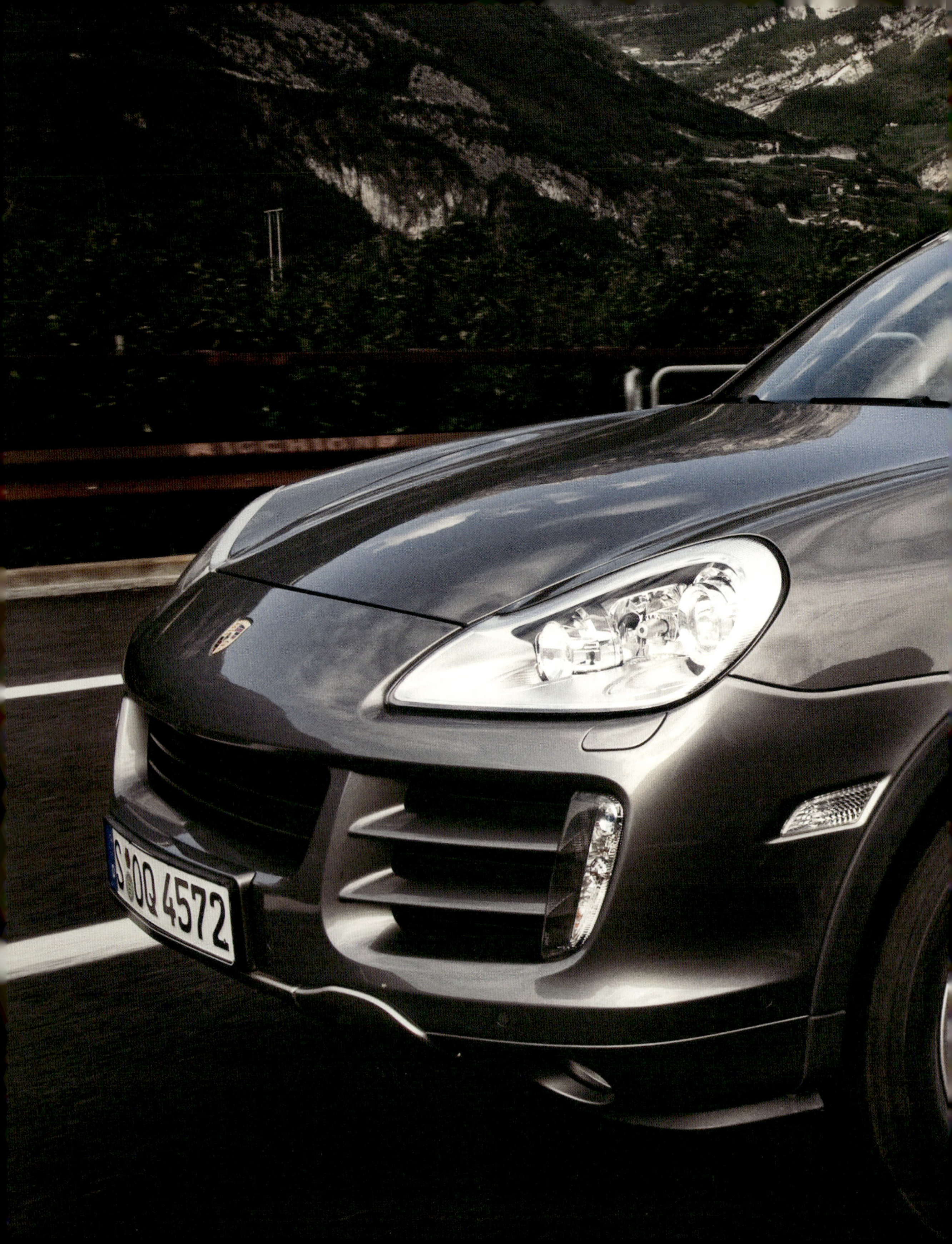
S OQ 4572

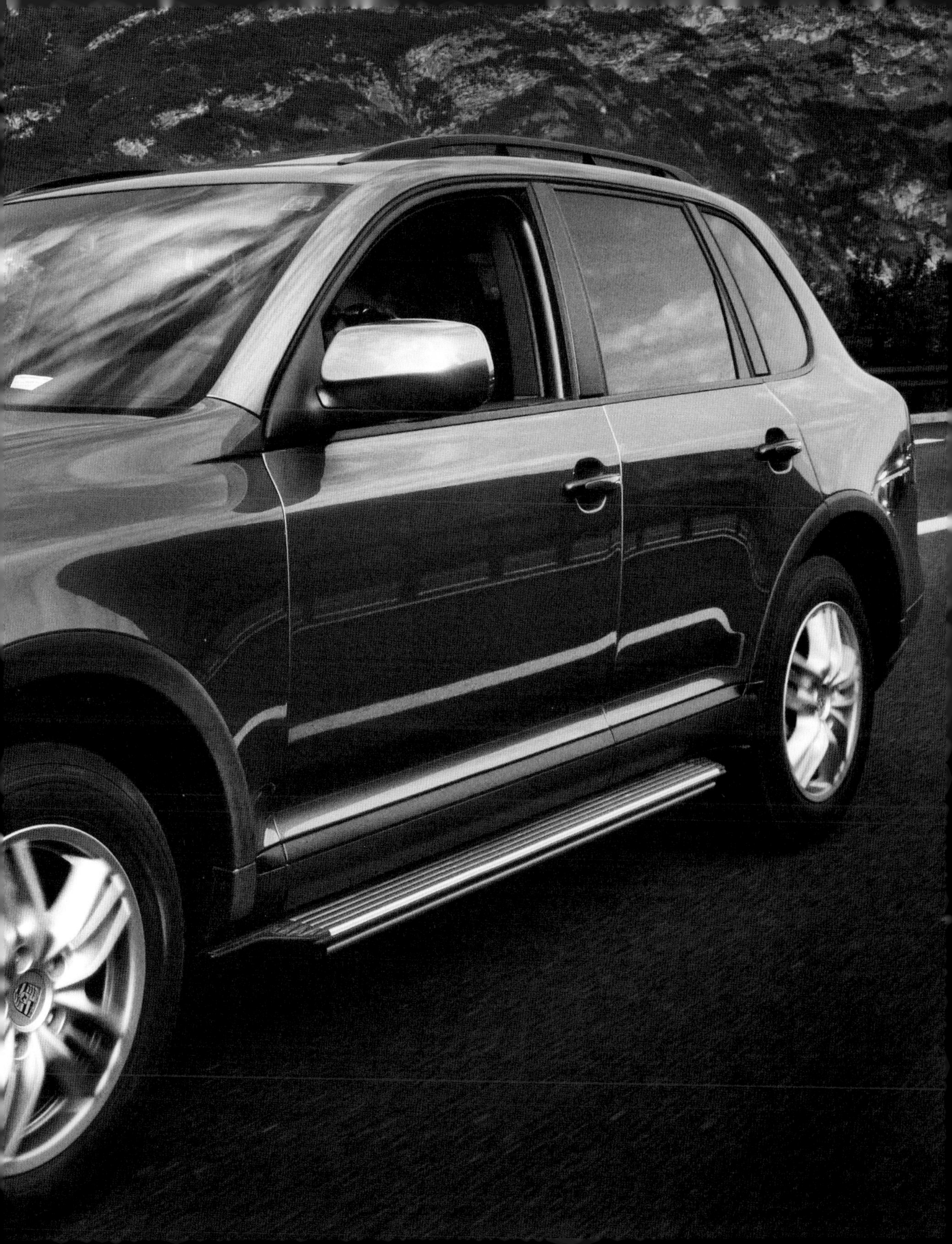

Easter Bells

Out of the blue the bells give voice,
Up from below o'er the ocean deep,
And pealing profoundly all rejoice
In release from days in the spheres of sleep.

From dull foreboding to this clear ringing,
From the very depths of the spirit's plight –
Heartfelt prayers are softly singing
Relief from the pangs of Easter Night.

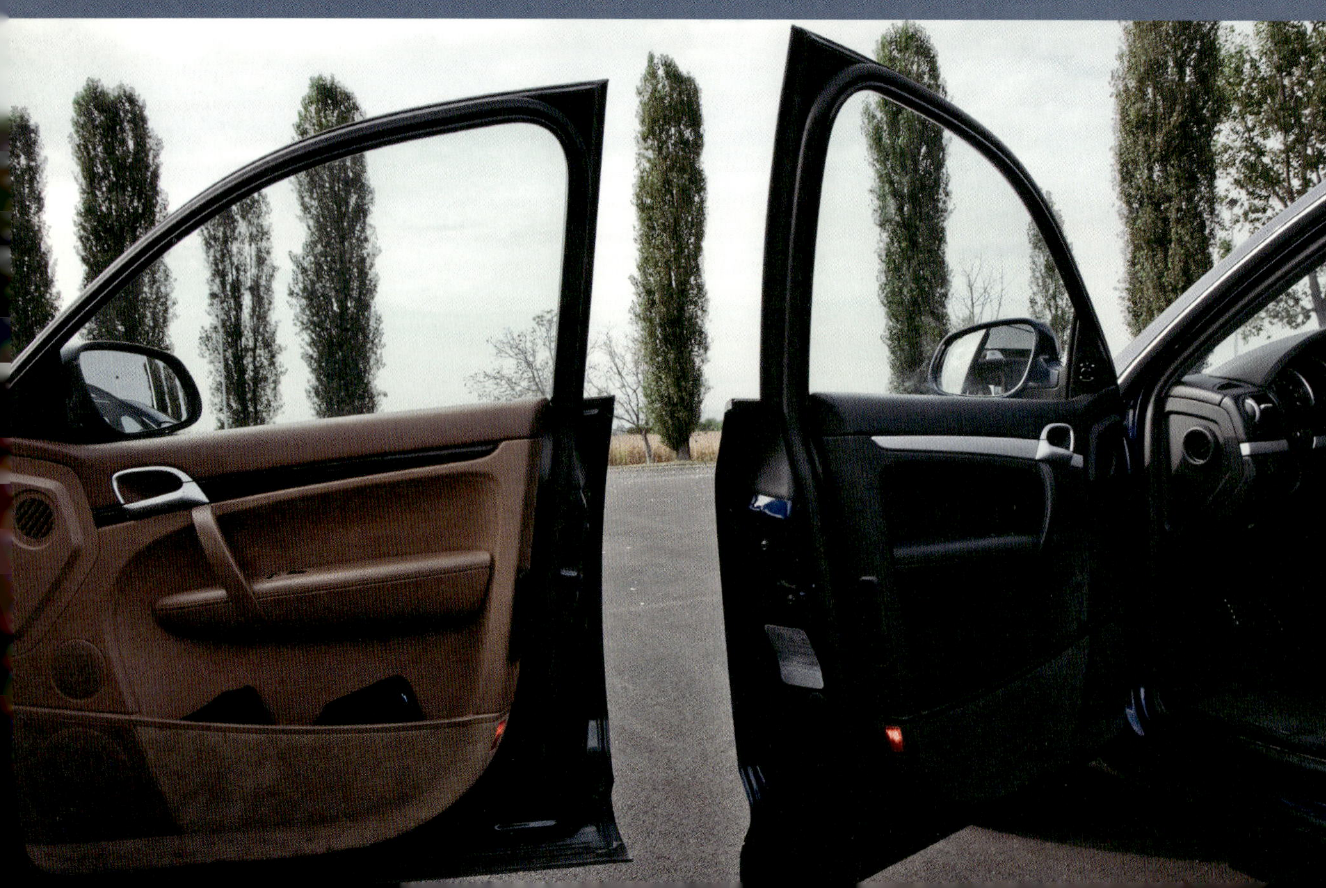

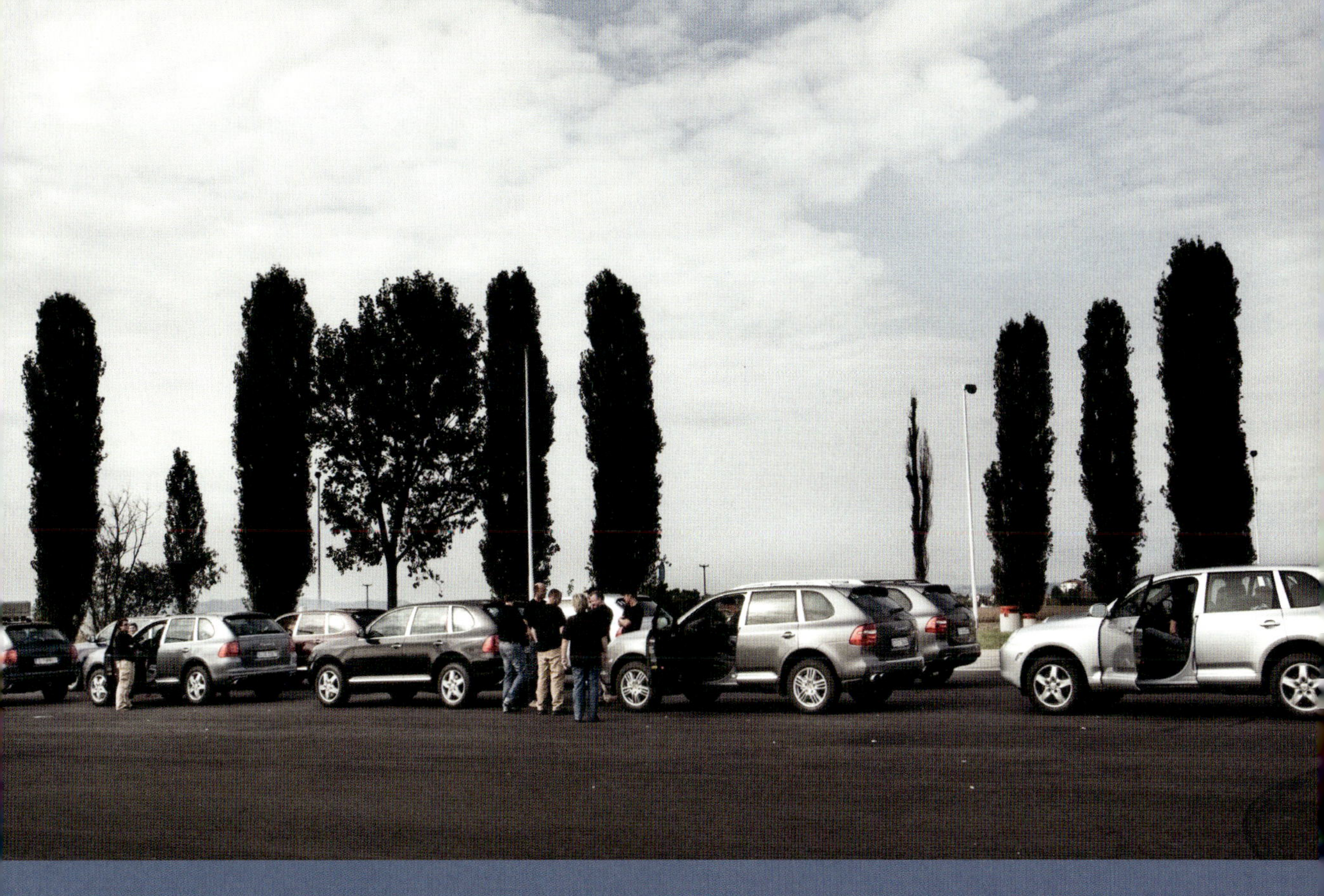

And now does arise a spirit so light,
Awakens resolve with a lively refrain,
Bringing solace and pure delight
For it is Easter once again!

Just Once

And peacefully the woods settle down
The fields and meadows are quiet now,
Empty the roads of day's to and fro
Free of the evening's echo
And life's ebb and flow
Swept away with the mist,
As if wrapt in veils of long ago,
Of purple moons and silver and gold –
All is far away and so far away
Is the distant time of old –
When suddenly, this:
Midst the clangour of bells from the valley
For once, just this once
I am seized by bliss.

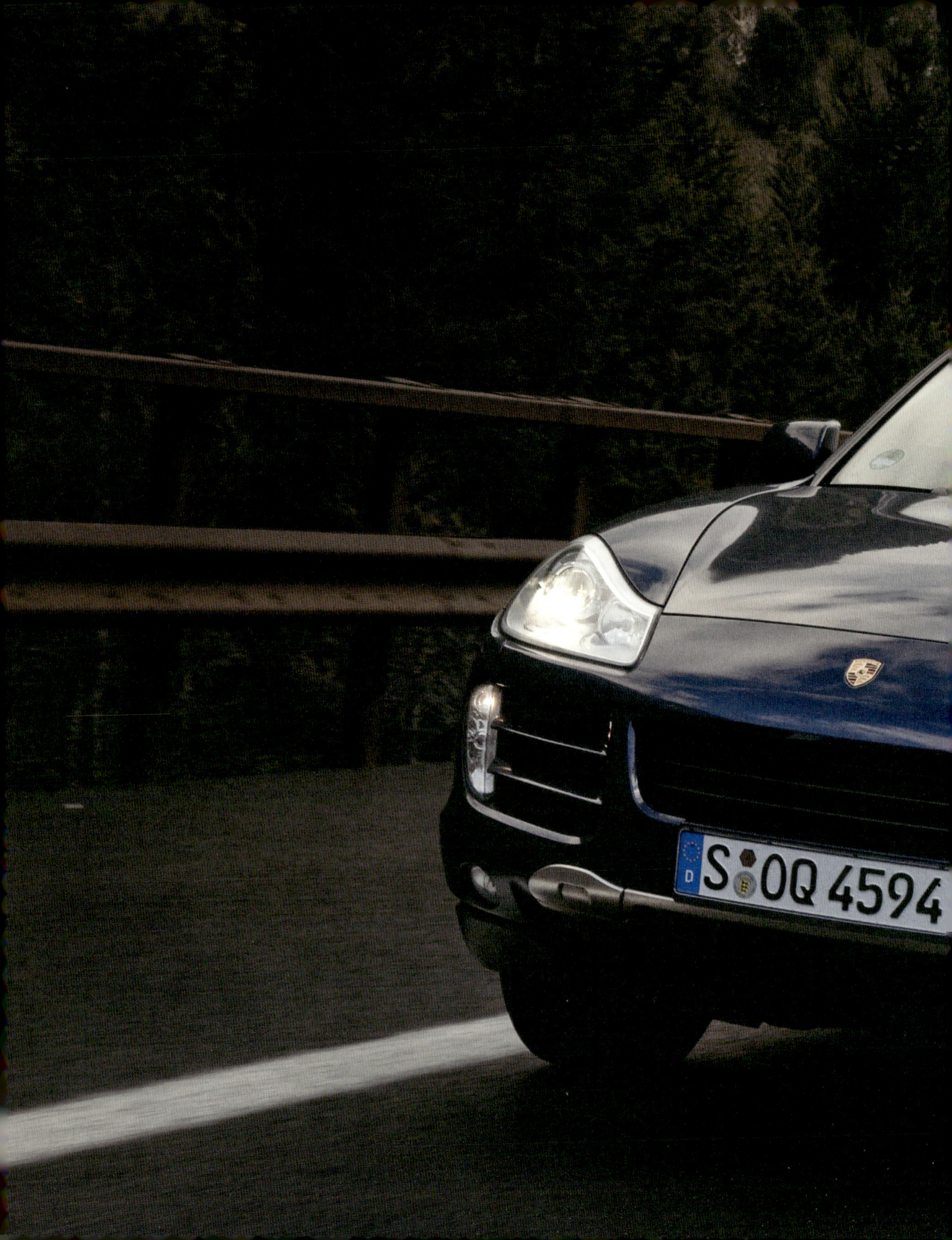
D
S OQ 4594

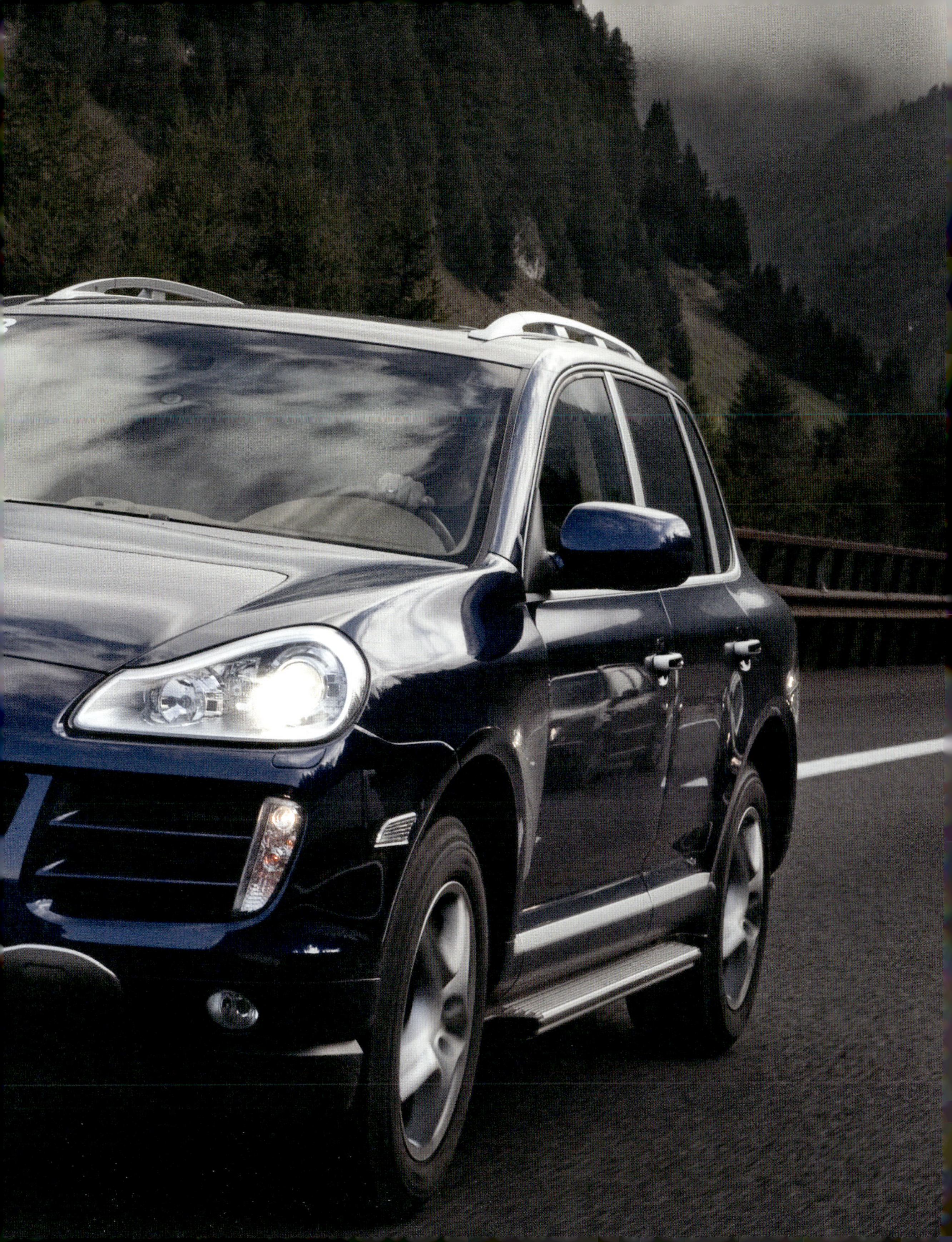

In The Night Dark

The wide valley lies behind us below
And the way ahead is jagged and steep
With sunset the clamour of men fades away:
Lone eventide on this untravelled road
Conjures up inward, reflective mood.
Night lays its cooling and calming hand
On boulders and over the barren fields.
Here the last tree holds itself solitary
In the shadows of a dark, dormant land.
But the road leads onwards through this night
And wrapt though we be in darkness and chill,
Issues yet from the valley, chasms, abyss
Weirdly wan and wondrous wraiths of mist –
Nebulous, hazy, casting sombre veils –
Concealing us from all human gaze
So that we may withdraw to an inner place:
The core of our being alone to face.
Alone we discern the soul's inner light –
Lost is the lure of the mind's distractions
In this one especial, singular night.
And through the darkness and through the cold wind,
The frost, the ice, towering mists unfurled,
Intimations now silently resound
Of other worlds that circle round our world.
From other sensory realms to us, lonely
Convey themselves, merging with human energy –
Forces, feeling ever attachment up here –
And among the rock fastness bare
Spheres of activity build and prepare.
Here is one way the true self to find:
Leaving the humdrum world behind,
For a time detached, new strength to gain –
To rebound then with rejuvenated élan
Refreshed, more mature, taking new heart…
Let us draw inspiration from yon way,
And travel on to do justice to our part!

As the weather modifies the journey,
so the mood modifies one's life.

Be a seeker in your life
like a wheel that constantly turns…

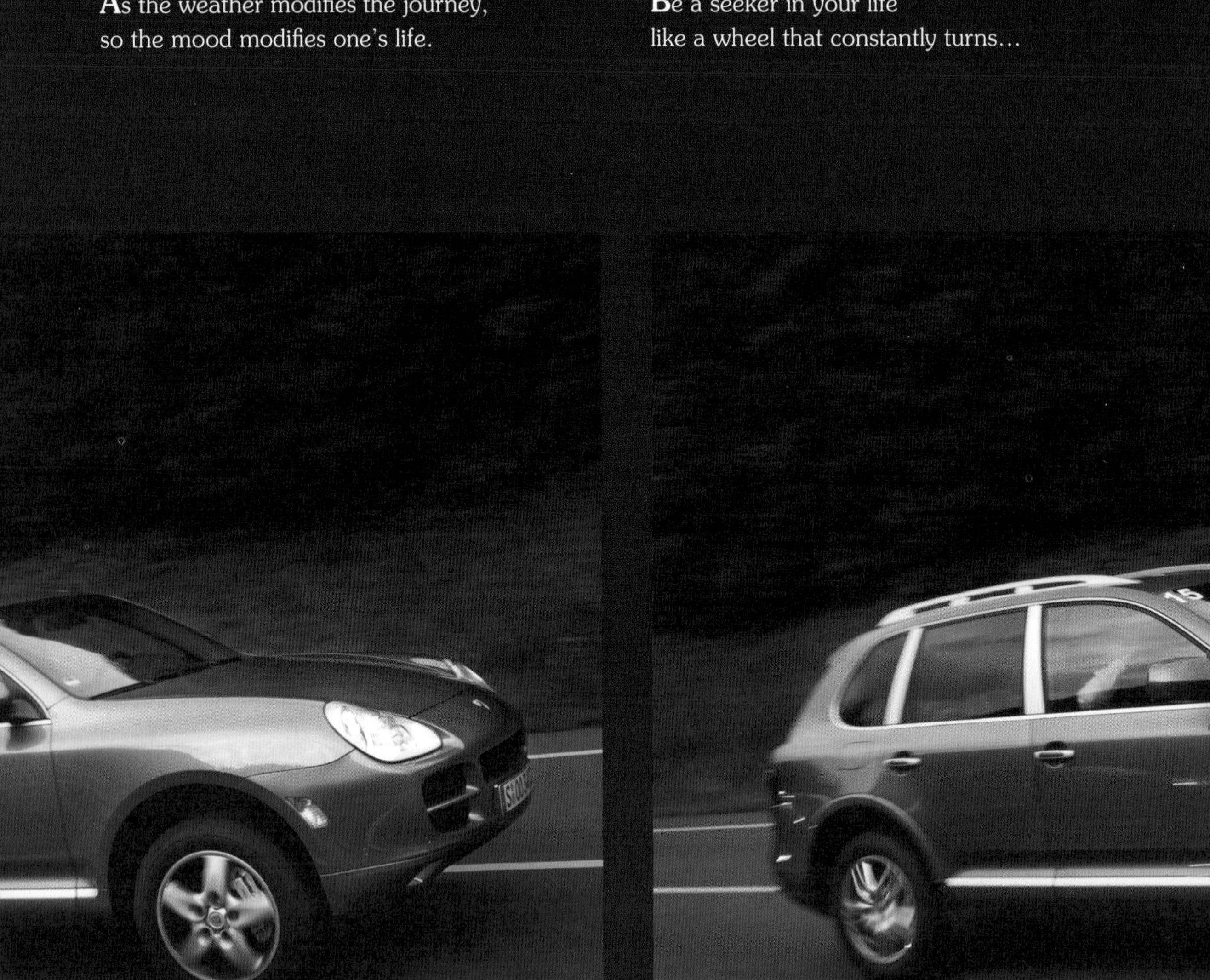

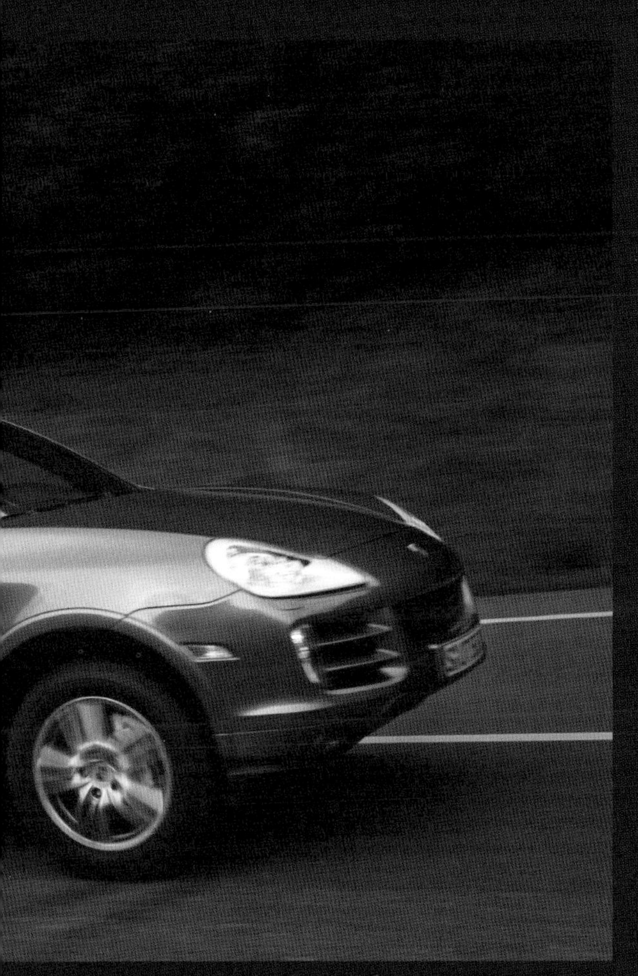

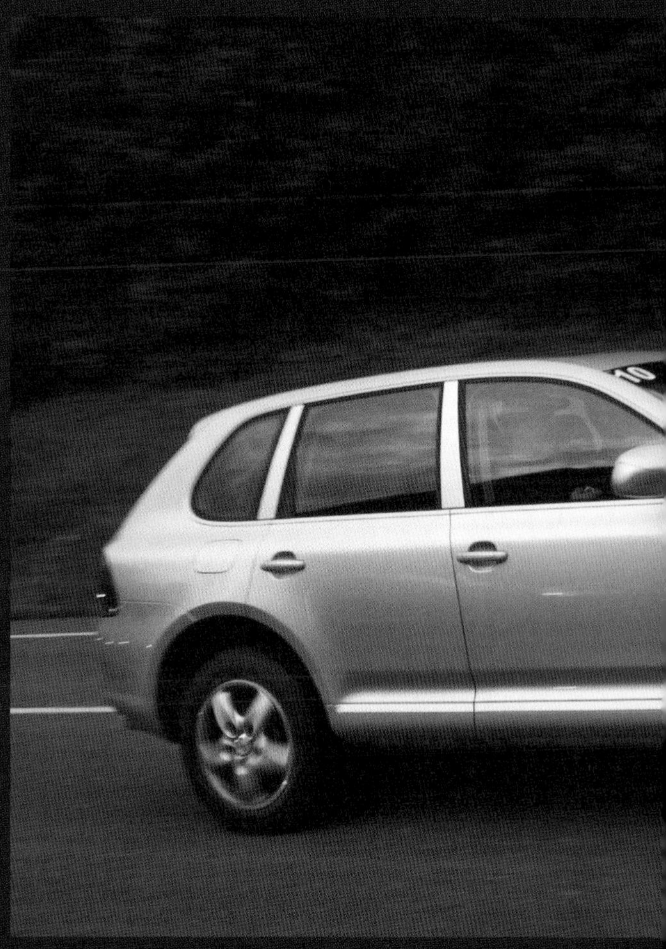

Heat does not only burn
it propels forward.

Keep to the steep road going up
and don't leave it coming down.

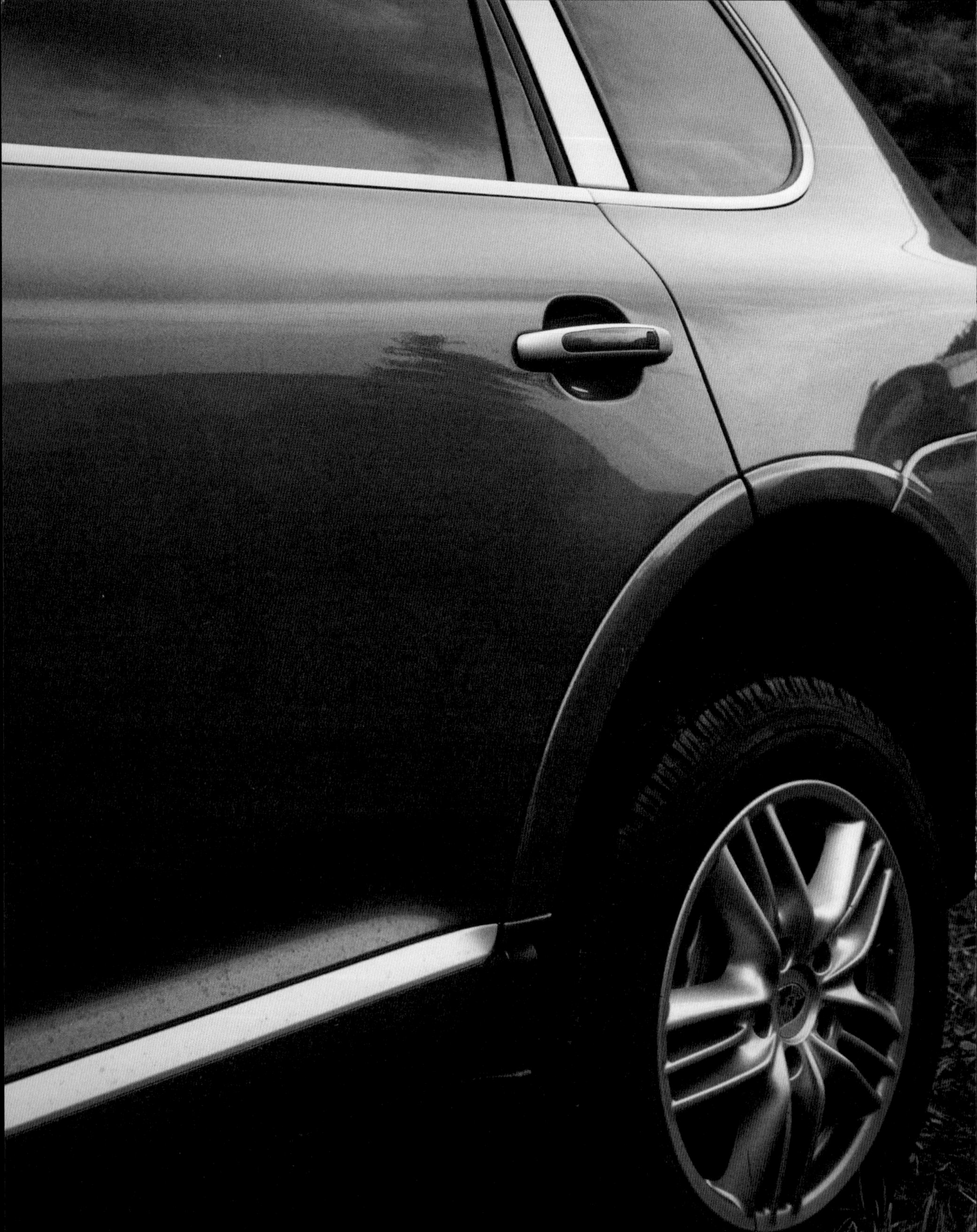

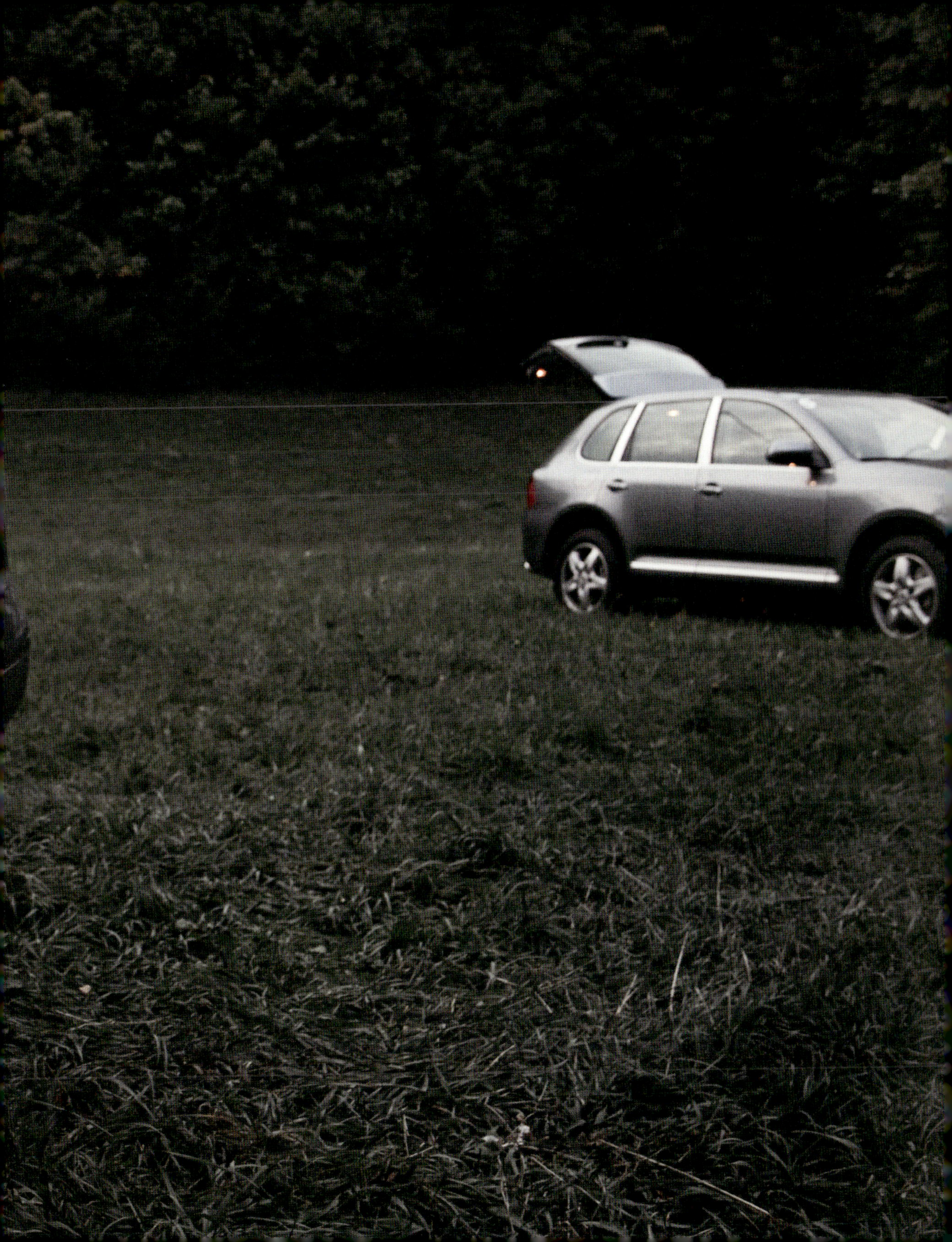

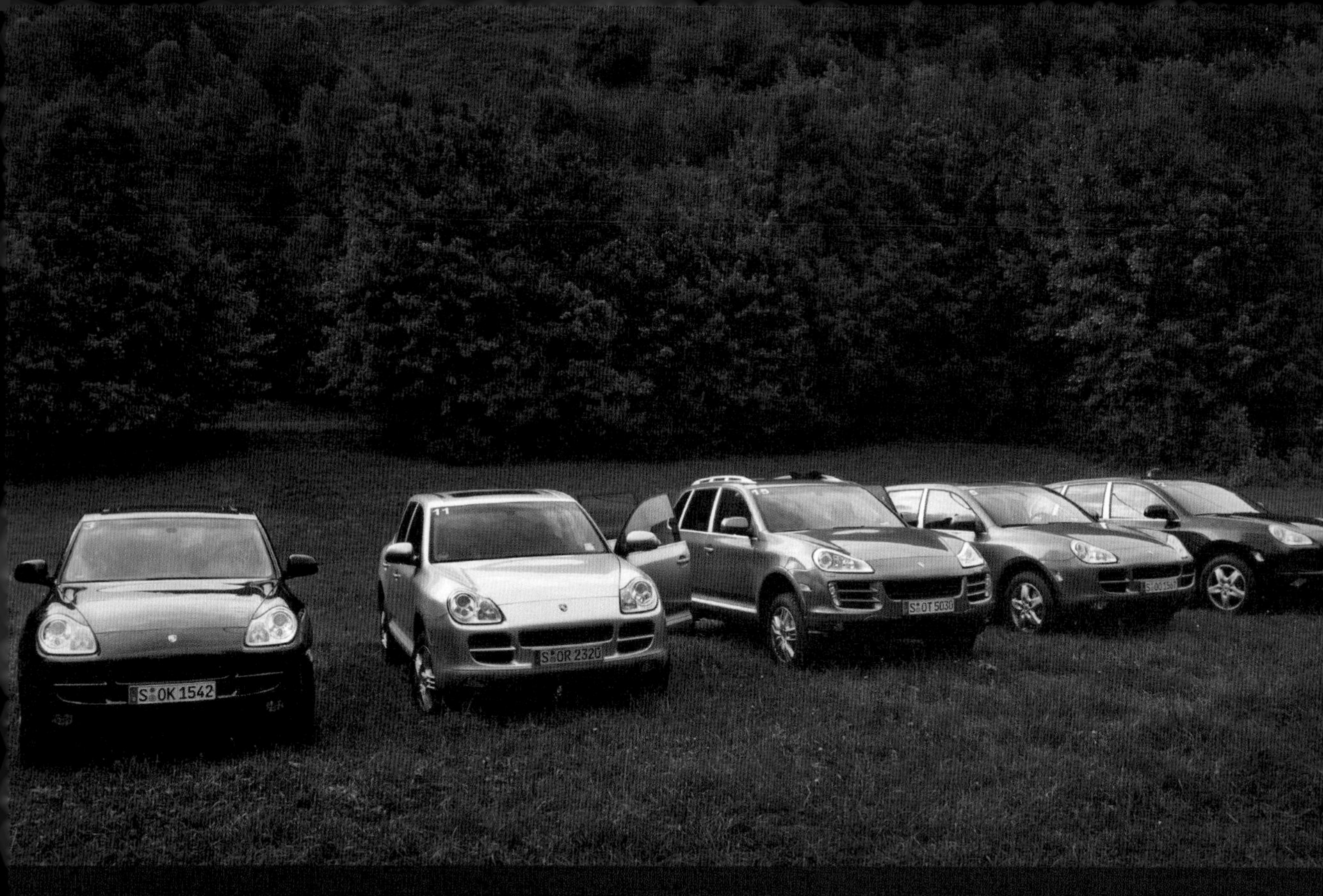

A Whispered Singing

Night has fallen,
All are asleep;
From the distant church
The bells are ringing.

Silent the wood lies,
While up from the stream
Peacefully rises
A whispered singing.

And now that night
With silence fills
The meadow and fields,
And the last bell stills,
So too in my heart
Now peace can reign.

In the brilliant aspects
Of faraway stars
The universe its halo reflects;
So mine forever is to bear
Life's joy
and pain.

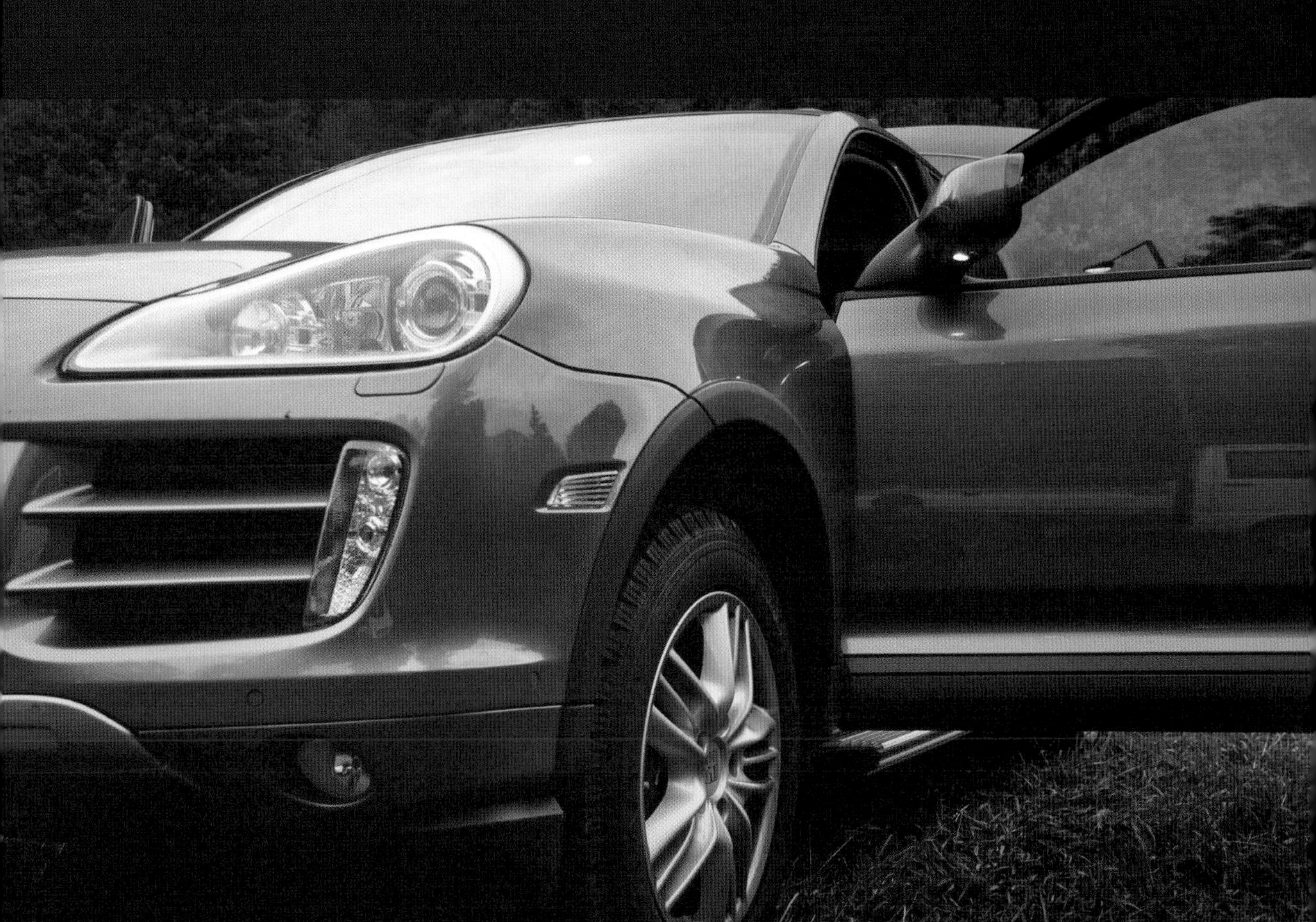

Nightsquall

Wild whirls the storm wind
Whips branches sere,
Racing from the woods
O'er the fields to veer.

Fierce whistles the wind
Whizzing through the street,
Sweeps the old away –
It's time
New times to greet.

Bold booms the storm wind
Till the beams all creak
Like thunder unfurled,
In and out of the night –
Off into the world.

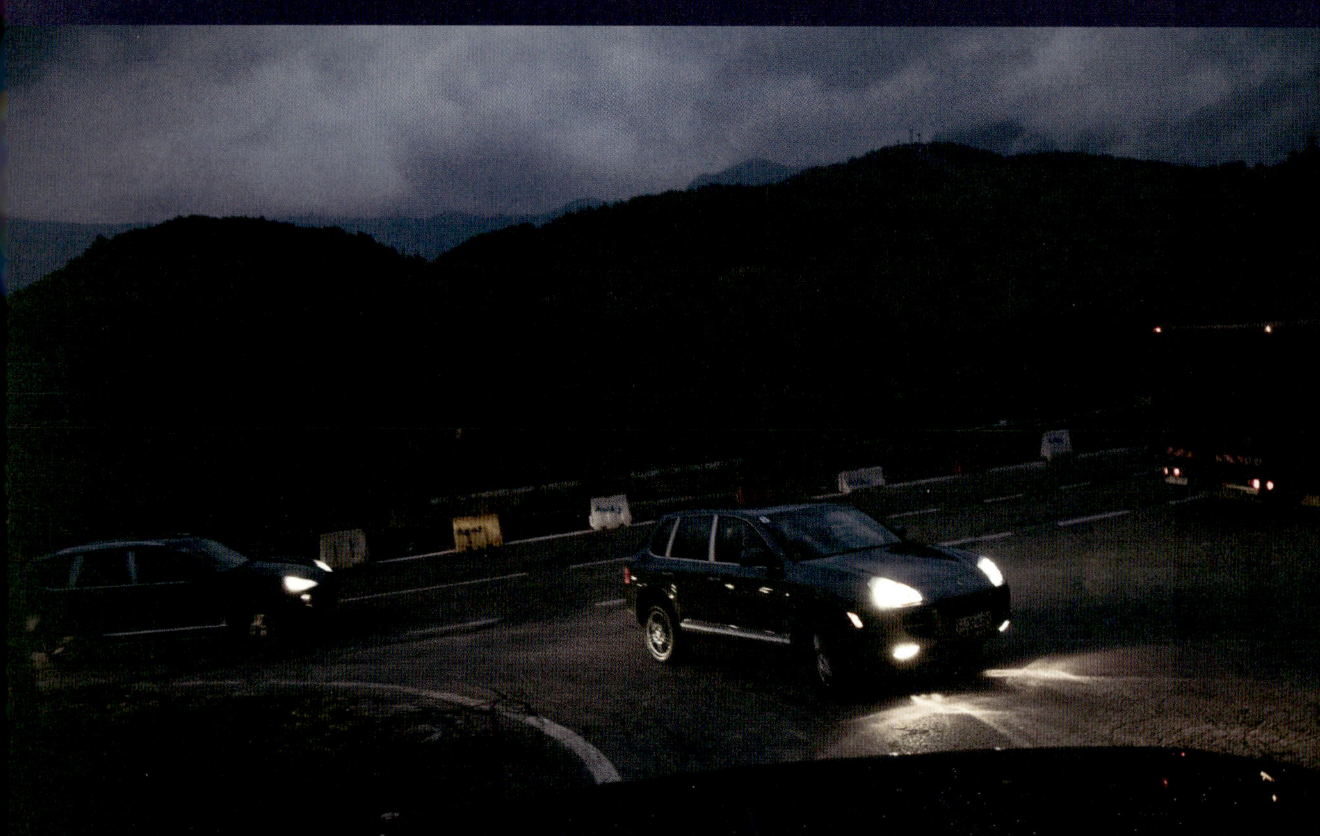

Full Moon Night

Tranquil, dreamy
The clouds pass by,
Friendly, sleepy
Before your eye,
O moon.

Your silvery sheen
Falls reverently,
The rustling woods
To o'er-canopy.

What calm delight
You reflect back
From flowing courses
Of waters black,
From the sanguine sources
Of night.

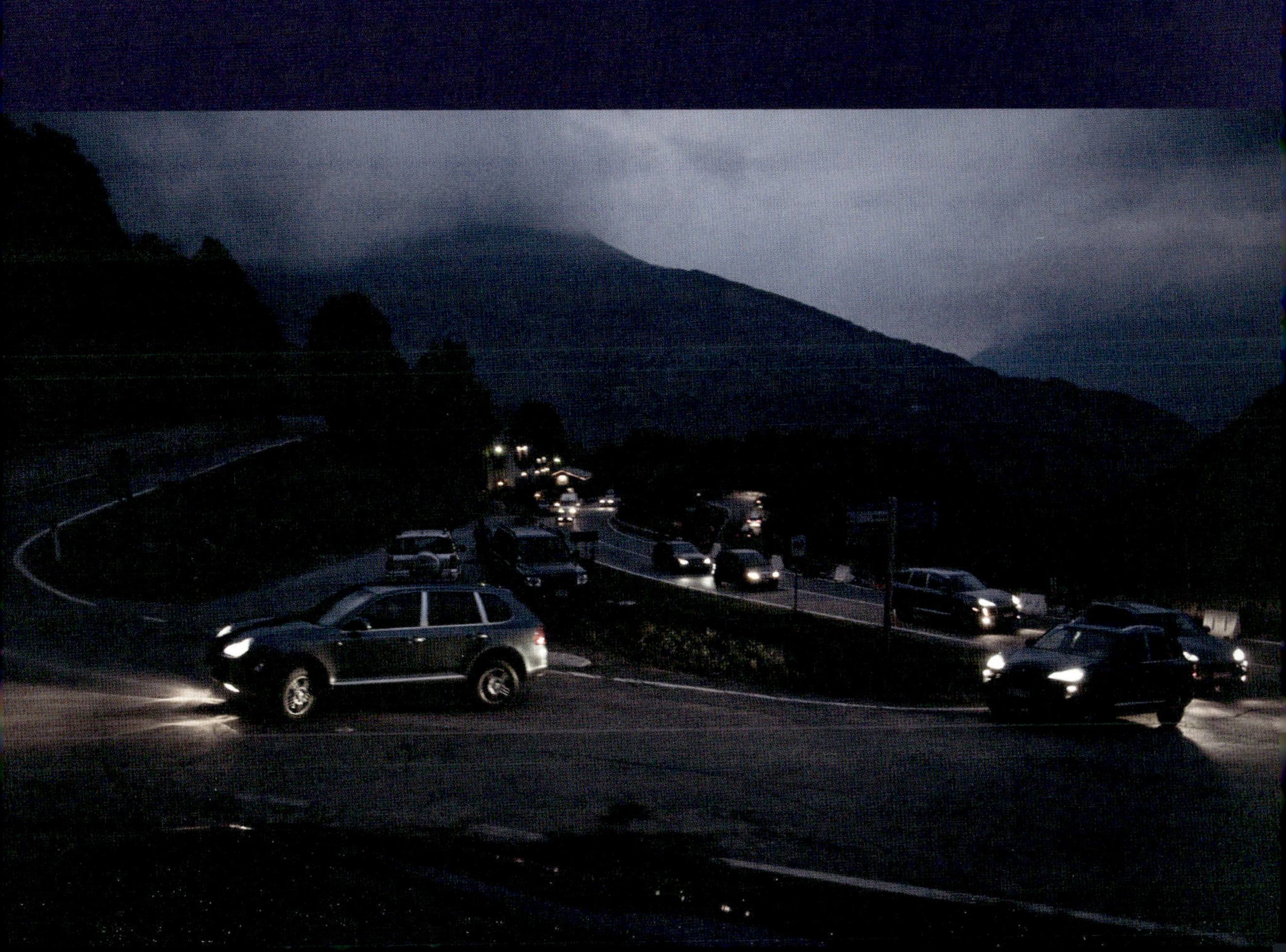

The Holy Stream

Down by the holy river
As it flows at the forest-edge near,
Grazing, grave, restrained and shy
Solitary stands a deer.
Among the meadows a lake lies
All crowned and swathed in mist
And a breeze thro' the branches sighs.

Down by the holy river
Strolls at the forest-edge, see:
A moose with antlers sweeping
Promenading with never a greeting,
In the sun-beams simply basking.
O to wander so blithe and free
Just from nature gladness asking!

Down there by the holy stream
Yearns at the forest-edge nigh,
Waiting and wistful my heart
And to you sends out this mute cry:
O your face is my thought's delight!
Only lift your heart to mine –
That the bliss of love us unite!

Down there by the holy sea
On the strands of the coastline streams
To the roar and the rush of the waves,
The will's unending extremes –
Regardless of time and terrain –
And inhales the calming stillness
Of attachment's yearning pain.

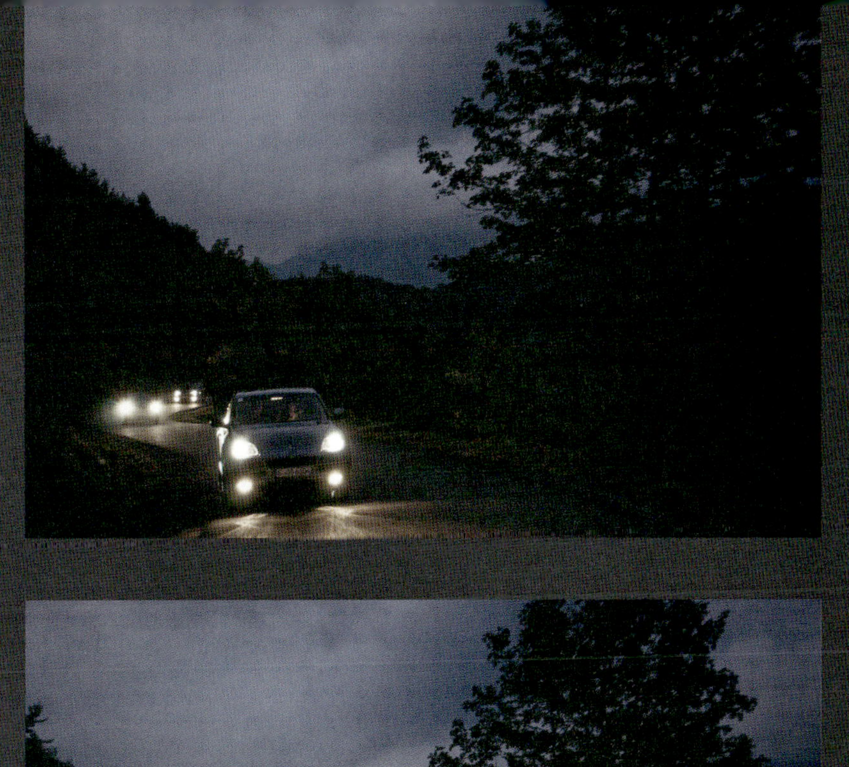

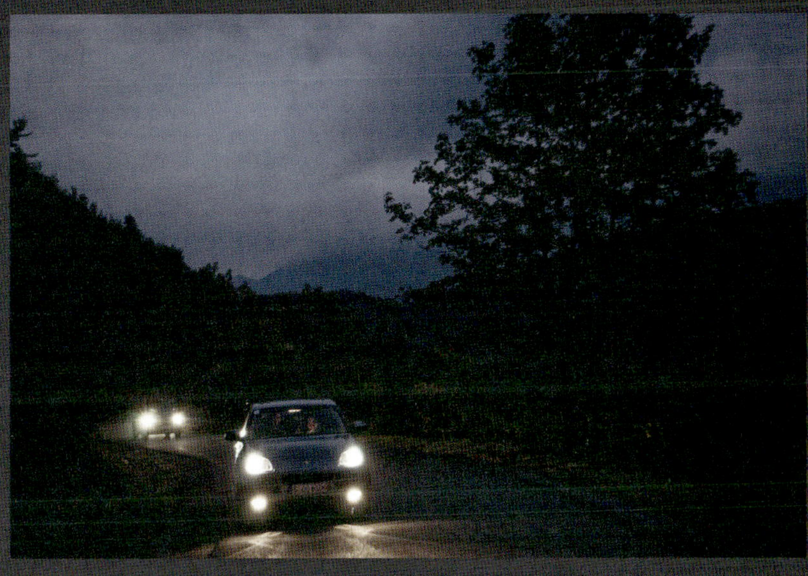

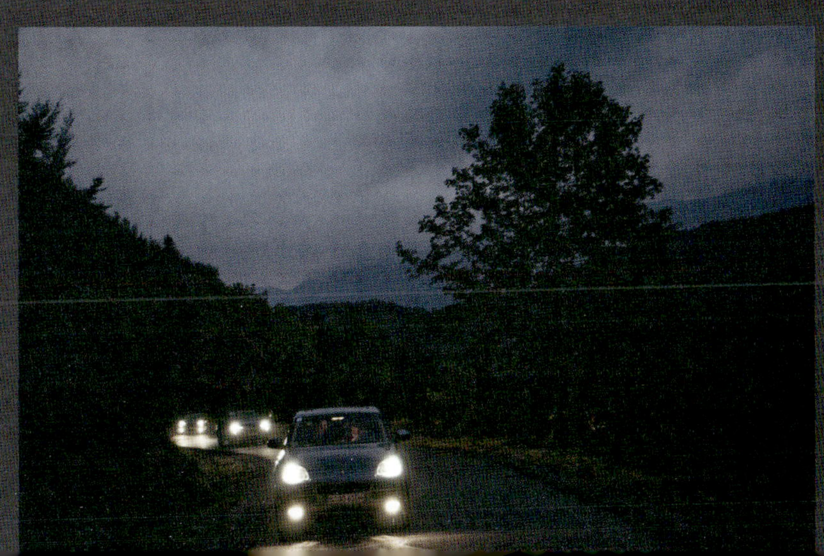

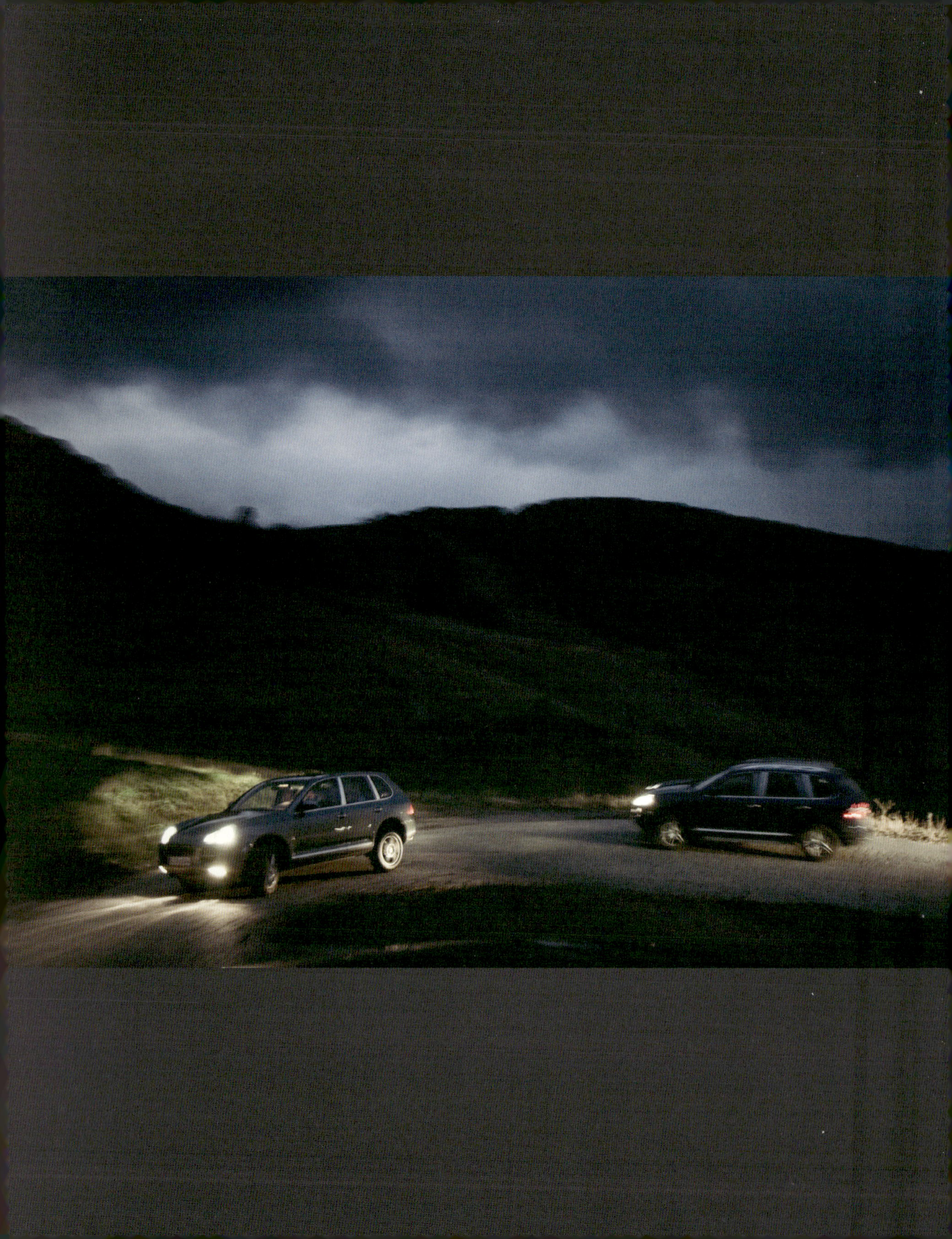

A Road

There is a road
And the road I take
Is my way,
Mine by night
Mine by day,
As long as I live
I make my way
through time.

There is a road,
There is always a way,
A way for me –
It leads me on
But leaves it to me
To find the way
My true self to be.

There is a road
And there is a way
For me all my own,
Yet as I go
Along my way
I am never alone.

Loneliness

It is a place
where nothing is,
truly
nothing more
all's set at nought
it's the abyss
of the soul,
where not
the least sound
is life-
recalling
only night
ever falling,
where day
is caught
where time
and space
have no place
yet spin
all round,
as in birth
or death
the first and last
breath,
unwitnessed,
where no judge
is found,
no start
can be seen
no end
sought
all is vain
every thing
of nothing
wrought
only living
for the end
there is no
aim
no sense
in this place
of ever
or never
of eternity
no trace,
there is
no hope
the self
to know,
neither joy
nor hate
can have effect
nor solace
nor rest
nor yet
bitterness,
a place where
life's glow
does not
reflect

and nevermore
does a word
the world
address, no
star shines
in space
nor worlds'

darkness
know a home
there and
only there
is the place

of loneliness!

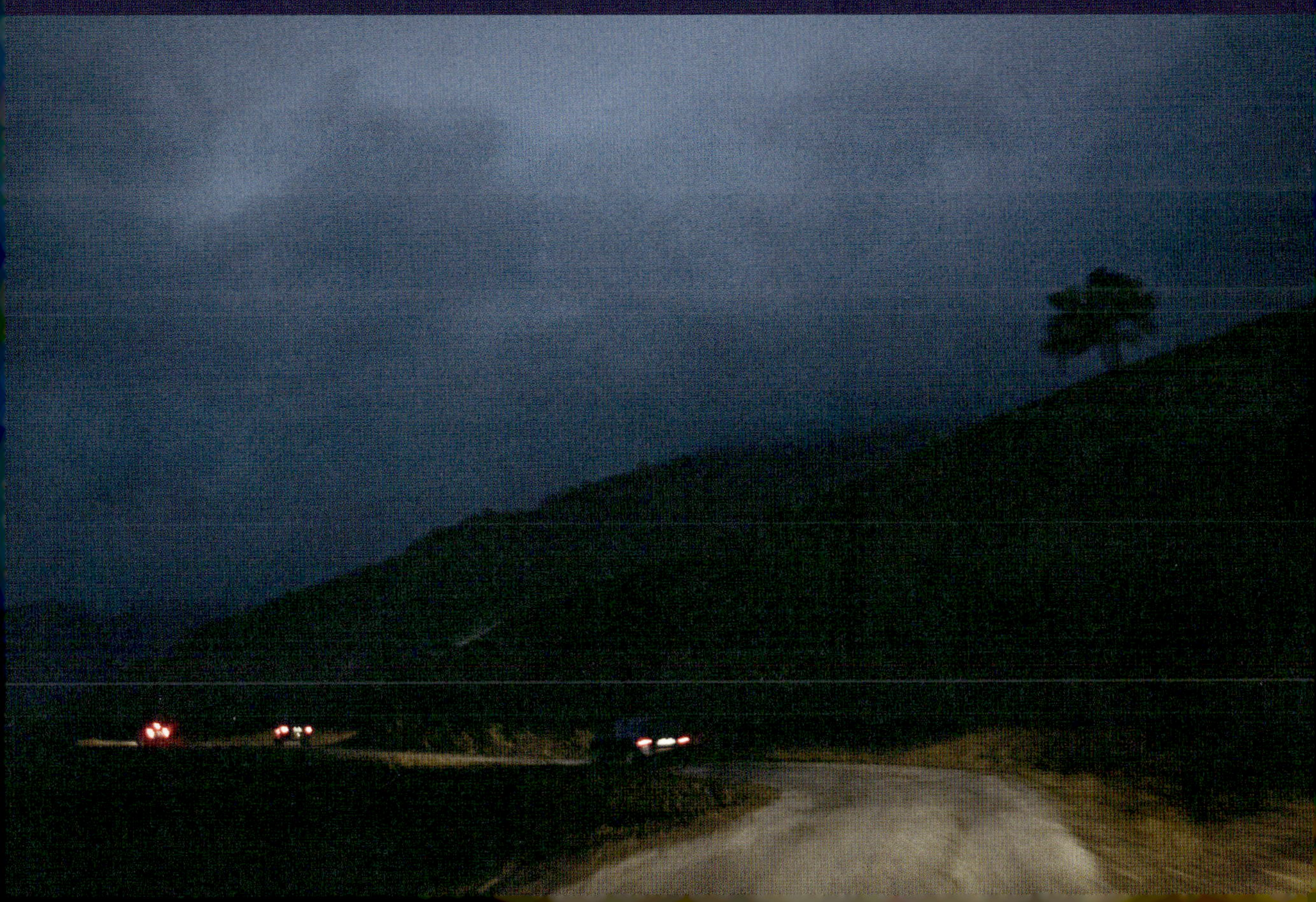

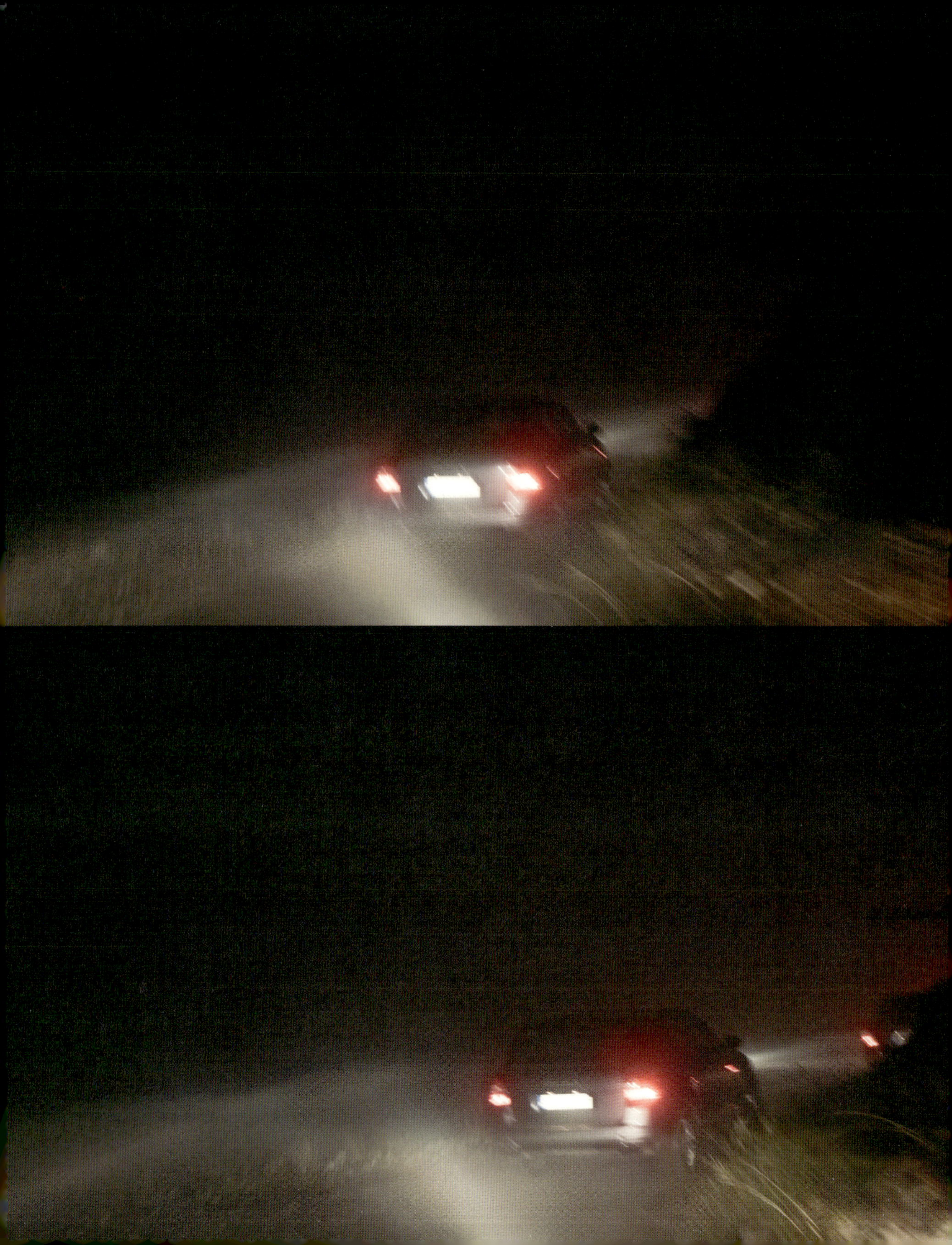

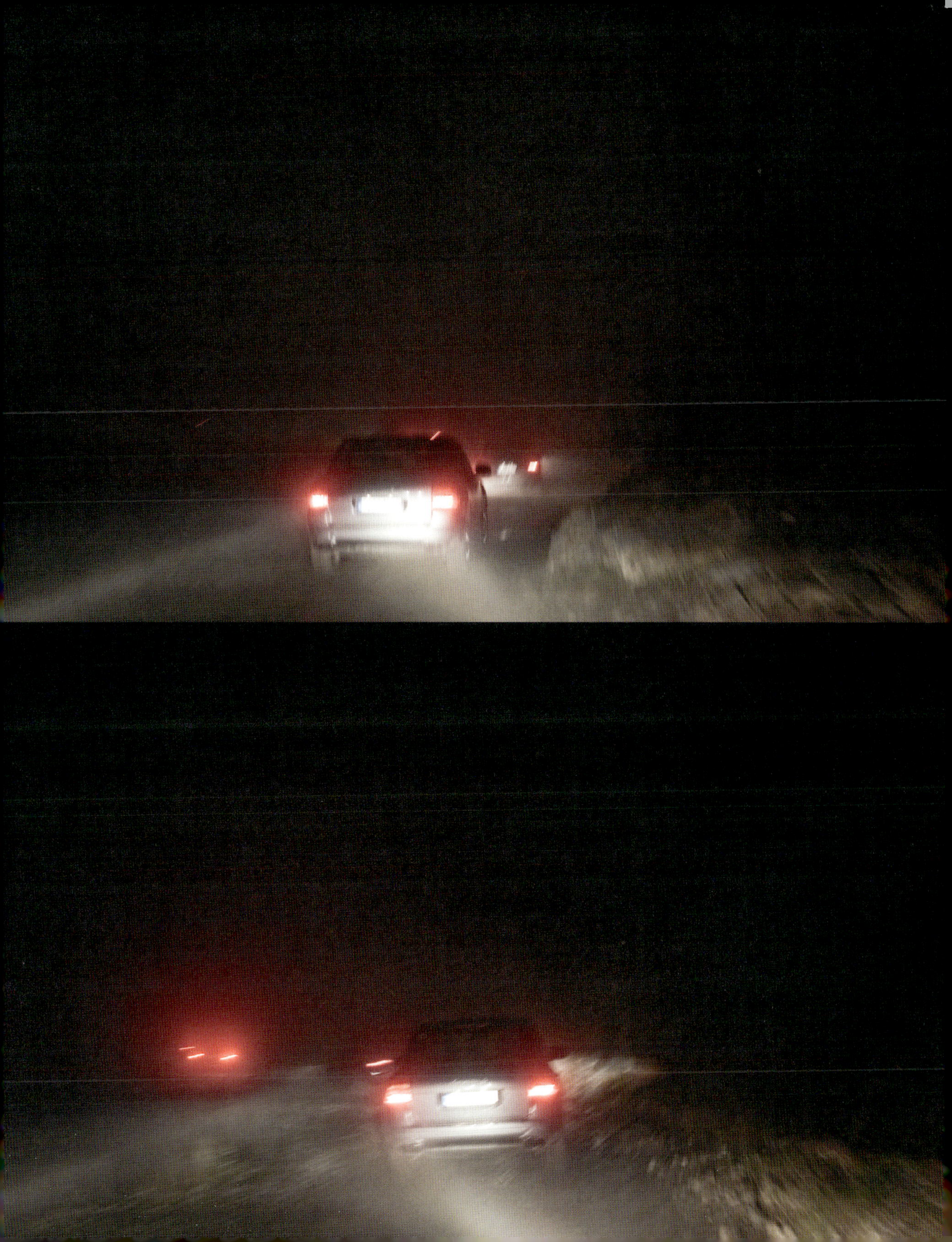

Wonderful Night

For wondrous,
Wonderful is the day
By night released
From its own dreams
That the night transfers
Out of sleeping worlds
To enchanted gardens
Where pensive silence
Unfurls.

Wondrous, wonderful
Is the day
That night
Of its tasks relieves,
To new being
Gives rise,
To a living
And seeing
As with wakening eyes
Itself does free
So that it may
The shaping
Of our time
Achieve.

Wolf In The Night

There's a wolf in the night
and it follows you, for
hunger pangs you incite...

In the cold of the night
the wolf's awful roar
leaves us breathless with fright...

And it's you they pursue
but before the locked door
they will never find you...

You they will not devour
tho' blood is the lure
for the light is your power...

There's a wolf in the night
and it follows you, for
hunger pangs you incite...

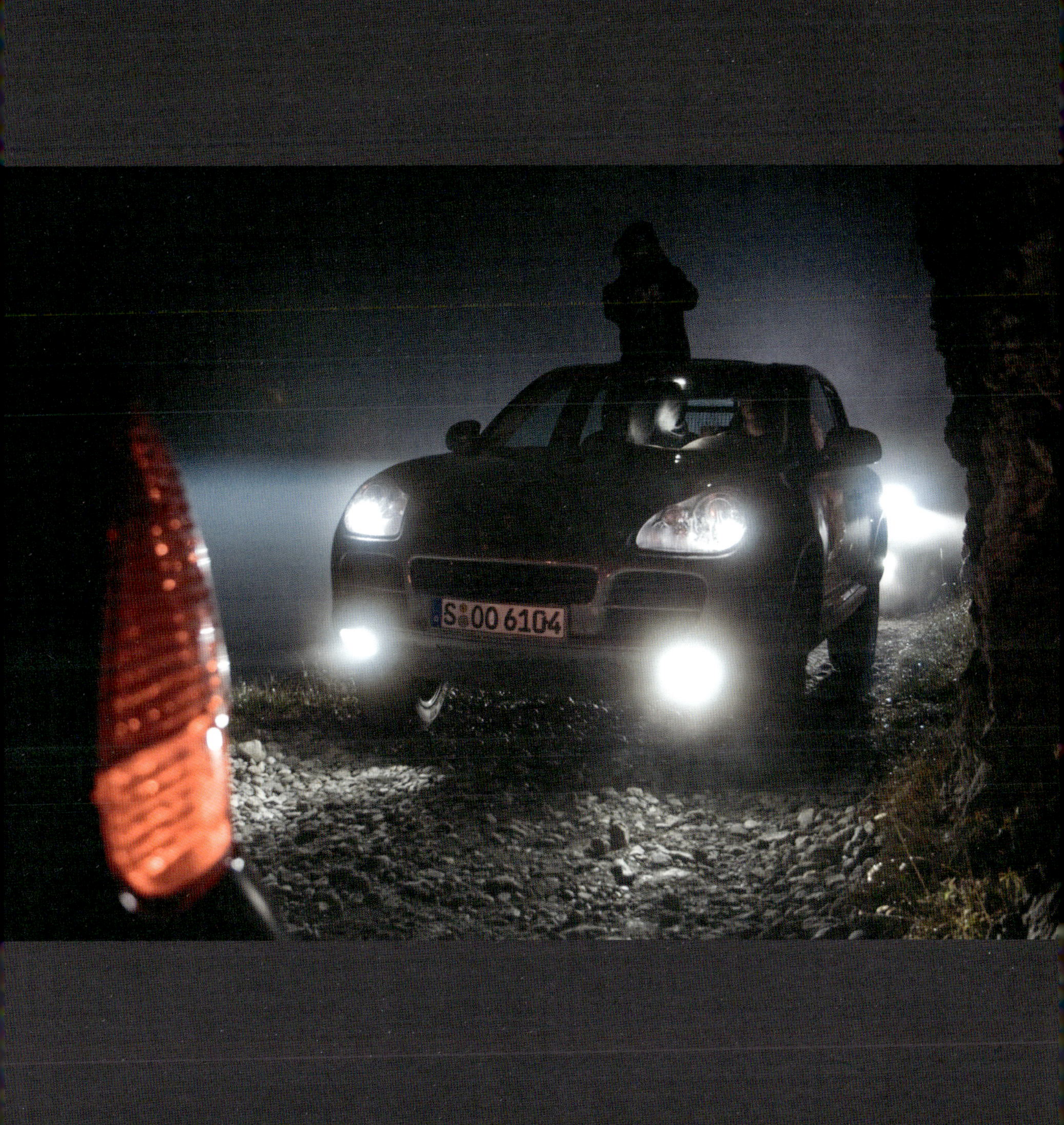
S 00 6104

The night was still and dark and deep
And softly drifted down the snow,
O'er empty streets enrapt in sleep
All heedless of mortal sorrow.
And window's flickering candlelight
Caused dim, ghostly shadows to fall,
When heavy steps passed out of sight
To icy doom beyond recall.

Beyond the village all was dark
Of light every vestige faded,
When out he ventured grim and stark
Beneath a hat his visage shaded.
Resolved this time not to forsake
The trial that once had been a loss,
His courage in both hands to take –
He vowed this one last bridge to cross.

Up the path ever further pressed
That haunted soul thro' drifts of snow.
Striving up with never a rest
Silently up the way from below –
To the high tower, looming dire –
Past apse and aisle and stalls did pace
And chantry, triforium and choir –
From the crypt averted he his face.

Through the door, up the spiral stair –
The narrow steps wound even higher,
As if his spirit to ensnare –
Led stone-encircled to aspire
The weary soul to his last rite.
The pressure grew with every breath
Once for all in this fatal night
The living to inform with death.

Step by step his way did he wend,
Intending in his misery
The night with emptiness to end
And from his cumbrous fate to flee –
To flee quotidian distress,
The unrelenting mortal pain
That ever did his like oppress –
And thus perhaps fresh hope to gain.

Midst spider's web and murky dust
Along the narrow masonry,
To reach that goal as soon he must
Aglow he strove the way to see,
Past proud arcades and stony piers
And up unto the main portal –
An end to seek to this vale of tears
Like many a despairing mortal.

The high portal, the last ascent
By such is reached with dull relief,
Oblivious of the last judgement –
Effaced the light of their belief,
Reluctant to their plight to bow,
Lost their grip on reality –
They hope the truth to disavow
Dreaming of fair eternity.

With one foot on the balustrade,
One hand cleaving to the railing,
Now he sought the plunge to evade
With a last tormented quailing.
Bemoaning life, ephemeral, brief
From very birth till final cry
Once more of sin he sensed the grief
But this blame too is soon to die.

Now from below he felt the pull,
Swooning, strained the void to embrace
As if with hope the depths were full –
Offering relief from life's disgrace,
Piercing his senses through and through.
Shrug off life's shackles he who dare –
Tho' freed forever from hurdles new –
The "Day of Reckoning" beware!

Just as his hand let go it's grasp –
Lo, from behind a pillar ran
And folded him within his clasp
The benevolent sacristan.
The kind eyes of this fellow being
Banished the suicide's despair –
Rescue he for the first time seeing –
As the sun rose in the morning air.

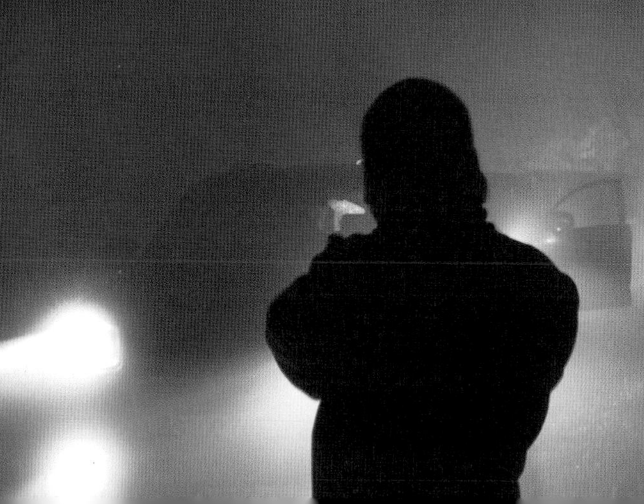

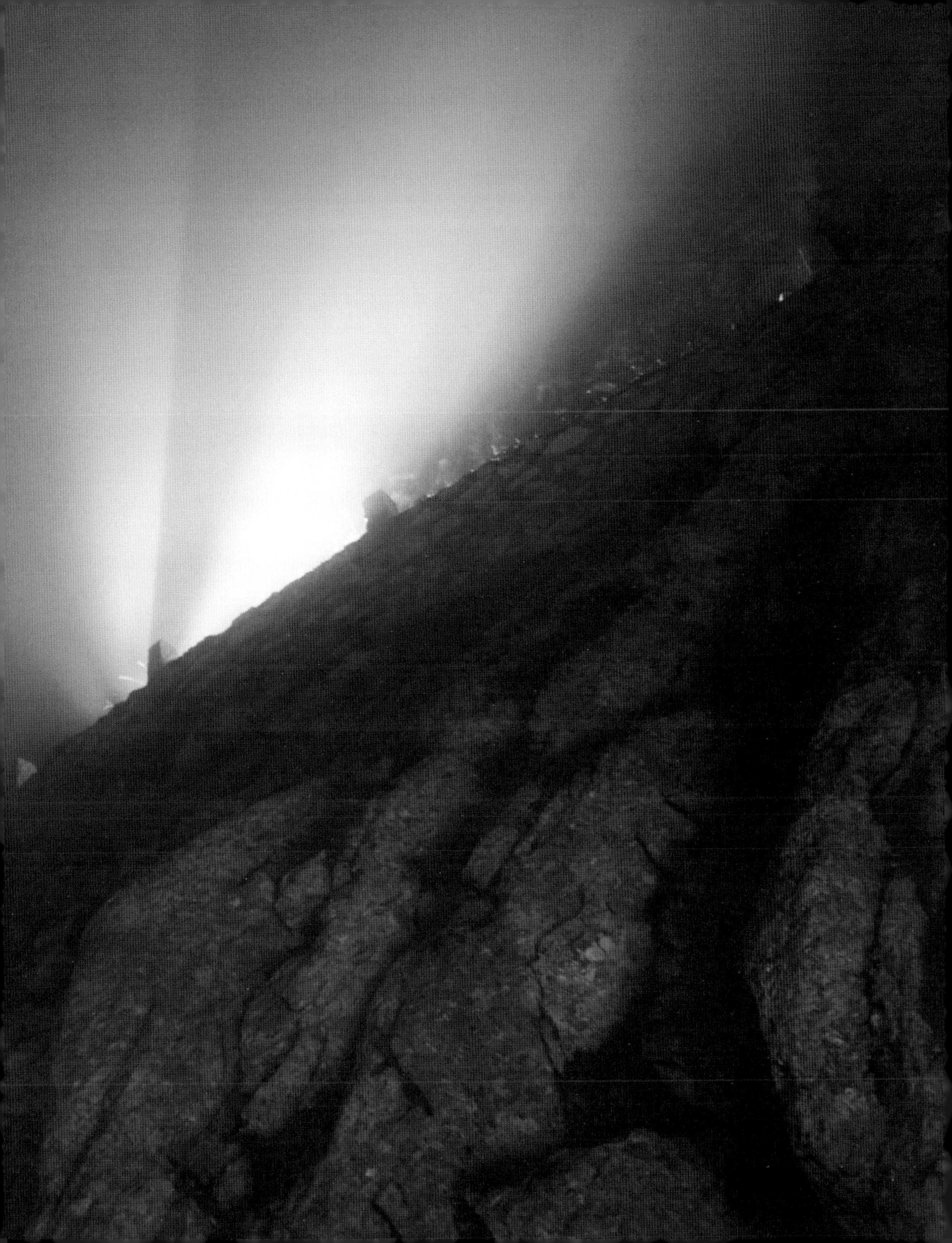

The Call Of Silence

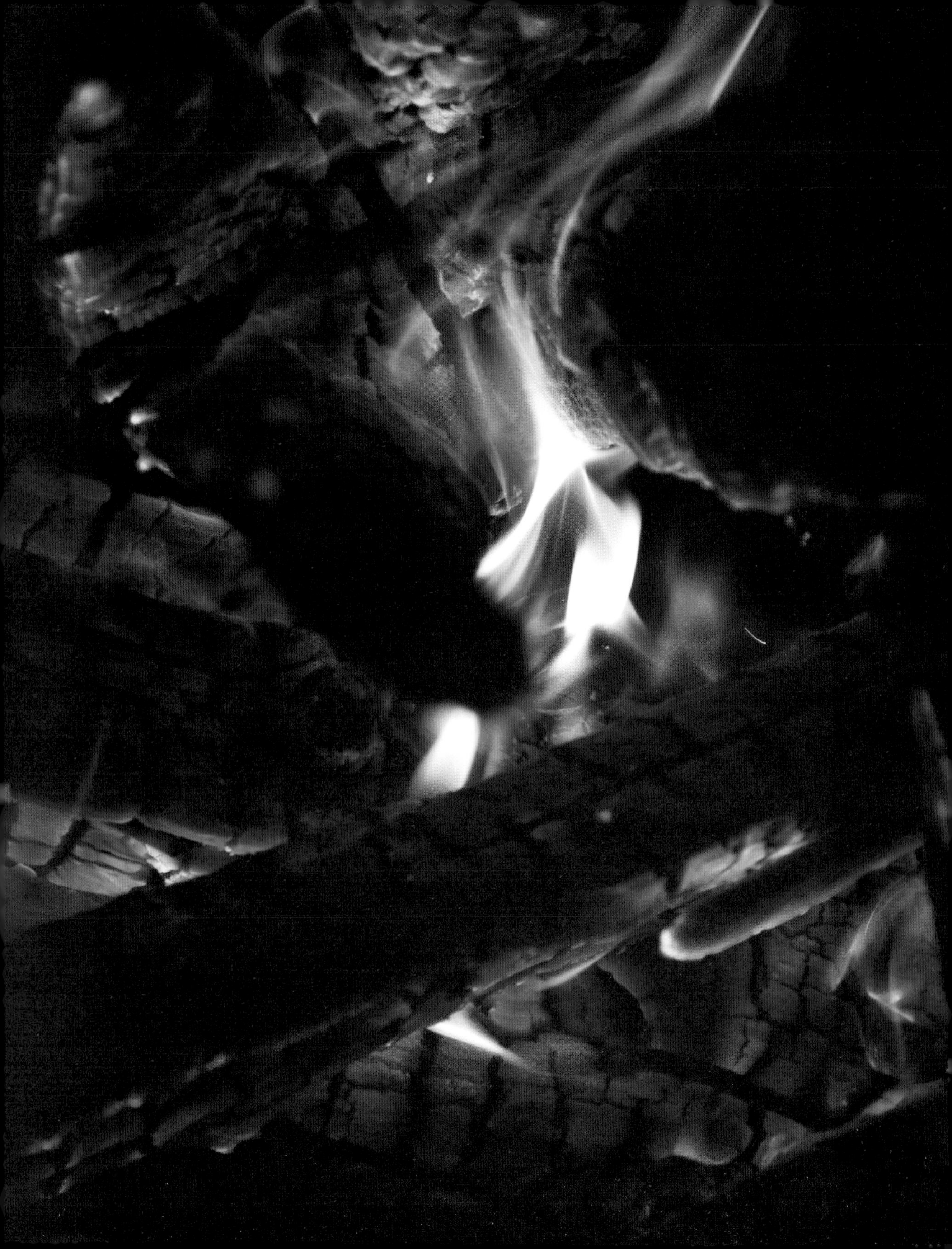

The highest point in black, deep night attained,
Past ravines on the steep and narrow road –
No sign of life here in these realms aloft
With freezing cold air, ice and snow and frost –
A sharp wind drives us soon to our abode.
There embers and the fire's last flick'ring light –
Where evening repast and a hearty drop
Many a weary traveller entertained –
Create for this short night a welcome stop.
And yet wreathes pale around this place the fog –
As in a cloud embrace
When the deep stillness of the night
Is pierced by the bark of the shepherd's dog

A bond at once is formed at this late hour –
Though cast up in a time of darkness here
With fellow travellers, kindred spirits now –
That we are not alone in life is clear,
As the firelight fades to melt into the night.
Now as tho' at the firmament's behest
The stars glow out clear and surpassing bright
Upon our warm and serene place of rest.

The last word is spoken, a human sound:
The biding of good night has been said.
Now silence casts its mantle all 'round,
The stillness has spread,
All is well… it is night.

Midnight Bells

In a dream appeared to me
A wild rough sea,
And it tossed my hair
With a salt dream air.

In a dream before my eyes
A cliff seemed to rise,
From the spume to emerge,
Sheer heaven-ward surge.

In a dream once I could see
A far-off country,
And my heart seemed to soar
Towards that strange shore.

In a dream revealed to me
Was a violent sea,
And spewed up by the tide
A shipwreck I espied.

In a dream once I descried
A waste far and wide –
It was no time nor place,
Only peace in space.

In a dream I saw with joy,
A couple, girl and boy
Walking hand in hand,
Towards their long lost land.

In a dream I saw a light,
A face fair and bright,
A smile soft and true –
This dream is you…!

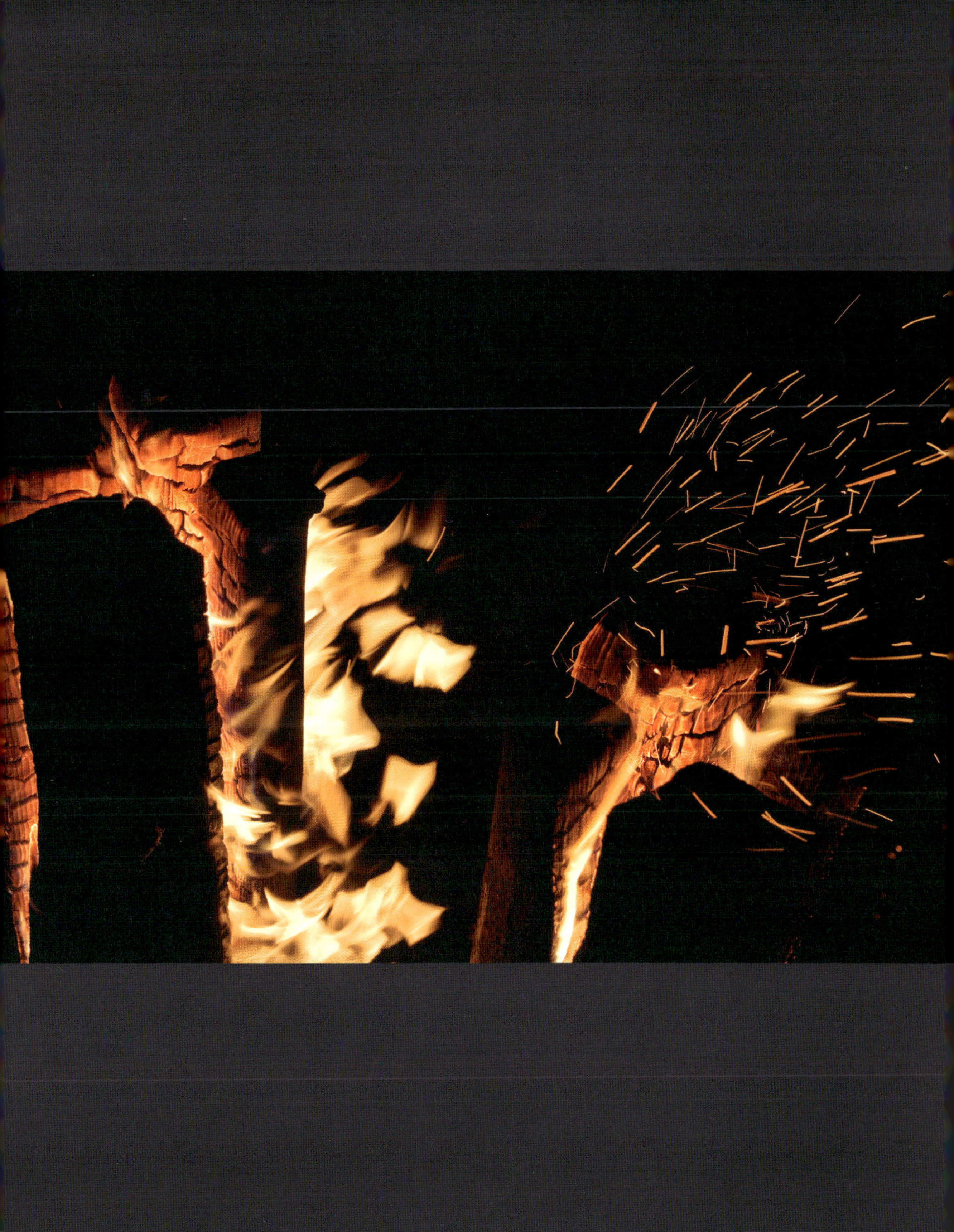

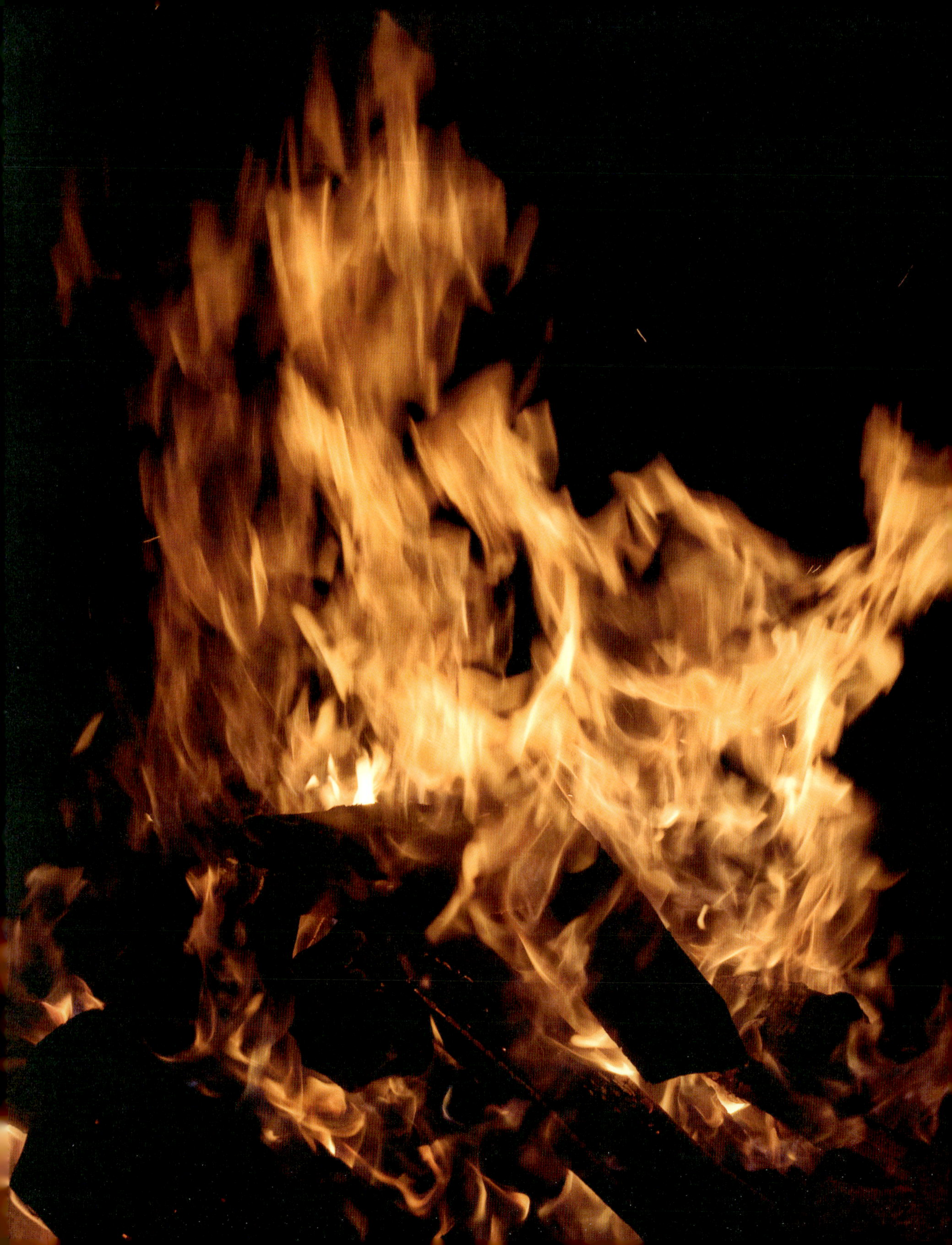

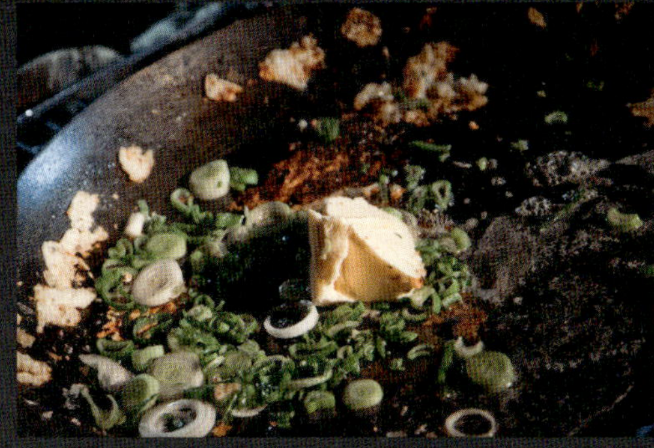

Treasure the moments of joy –
for times of despair.

He who can give comfort
will find it.

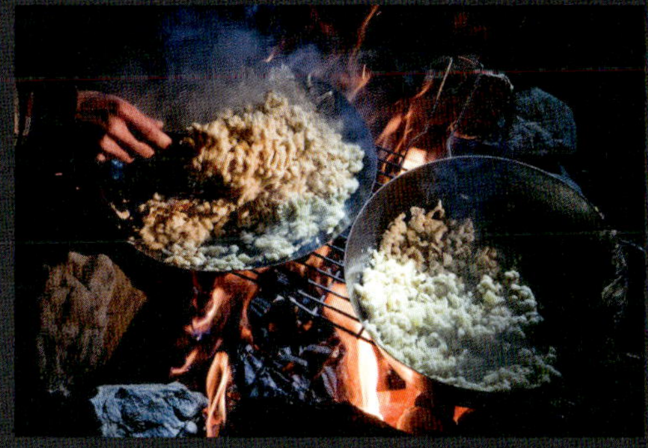

Never depend
on your happiness.

Movement is harmony
and language combined.

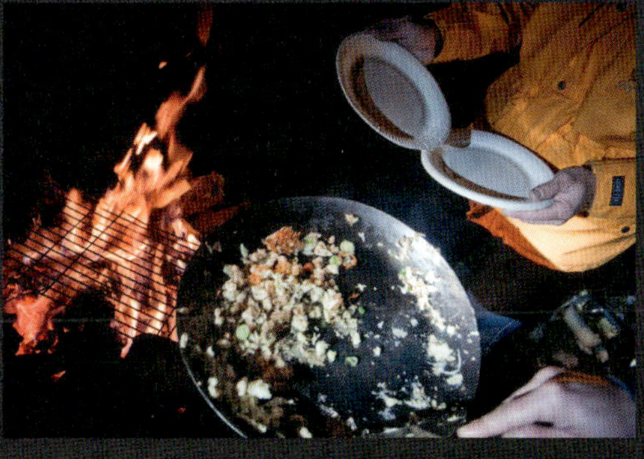

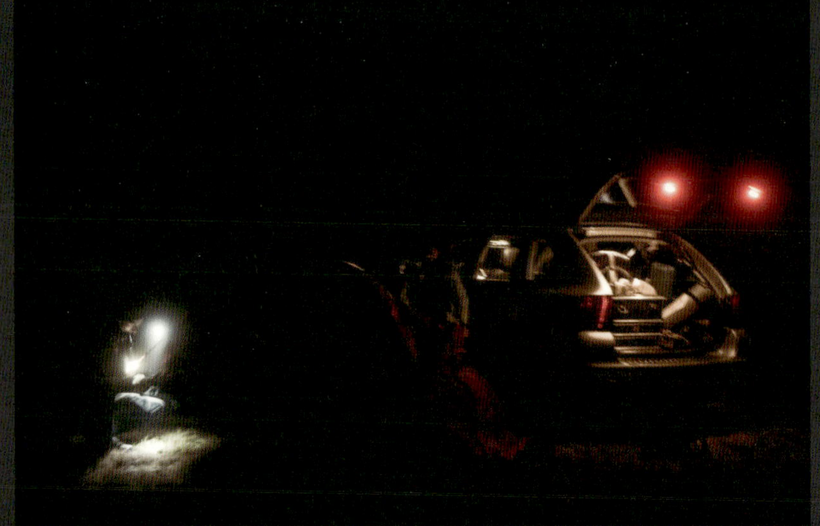

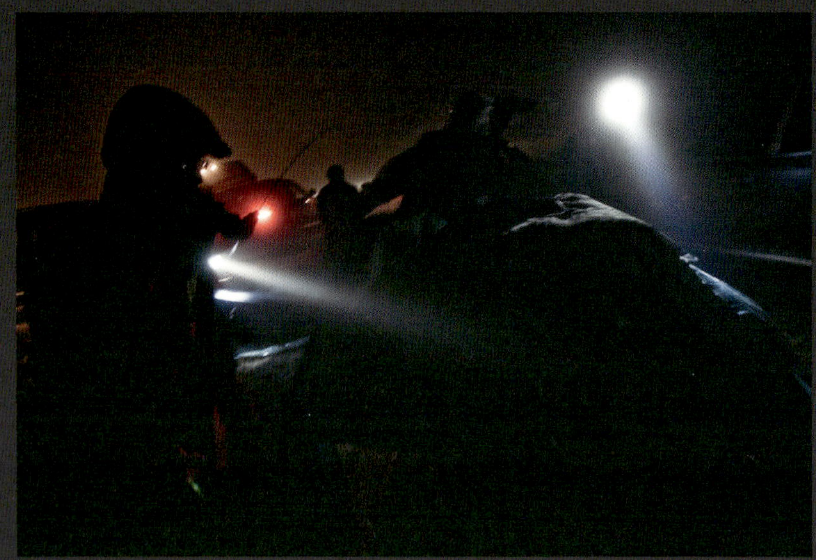

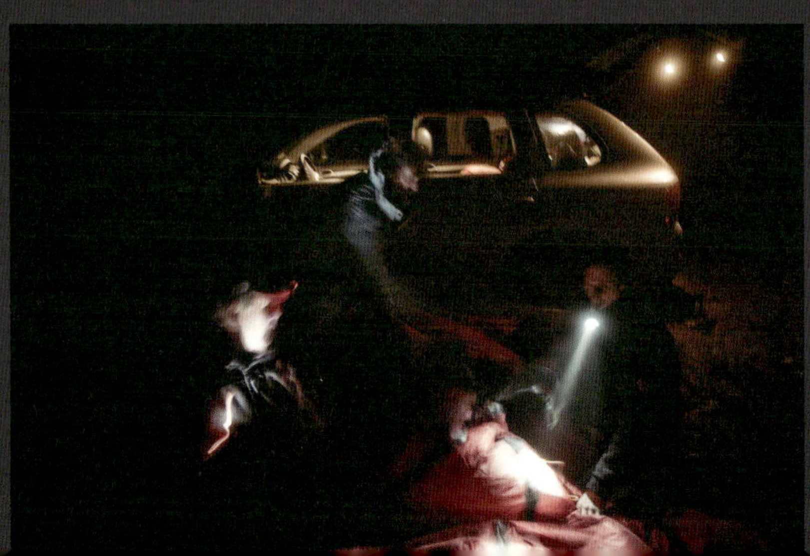

Trust

Here is my trust, I give it to you
I pledge it tonight,
I will see it through –
There is no end in sight…

Here is the trust in you I lay
This day I choose,
It will be my way –
A whole year for you…

Here is the trust to you I give
As never before,
By my life as I live –
Nor could ever give more.

Trust, yes trust
It has to be,
Trust in you, trust from me
Bright, pure and true!

Here is my trust, I give it to you
As this night knows,
I trust you now –
As my hope grows!

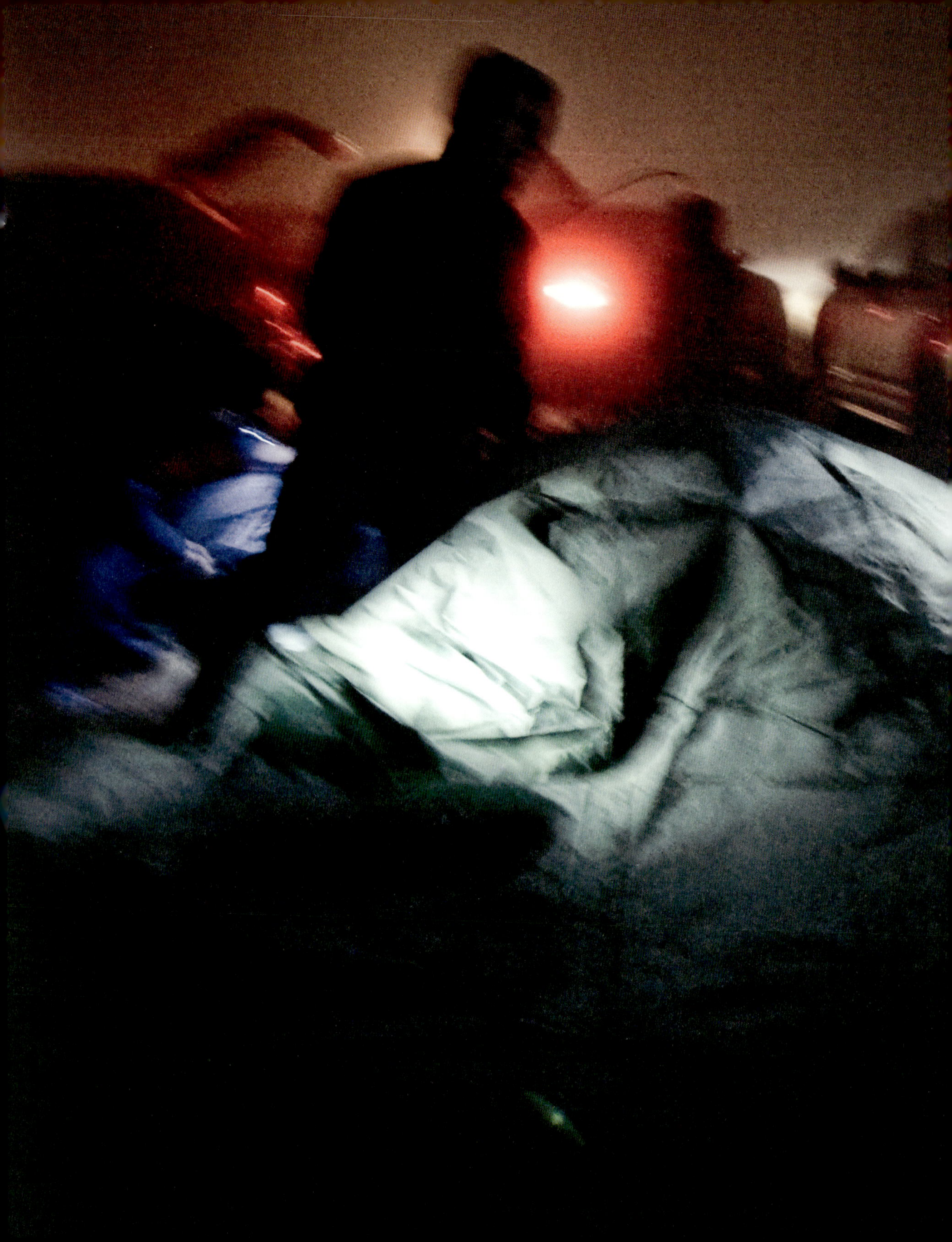

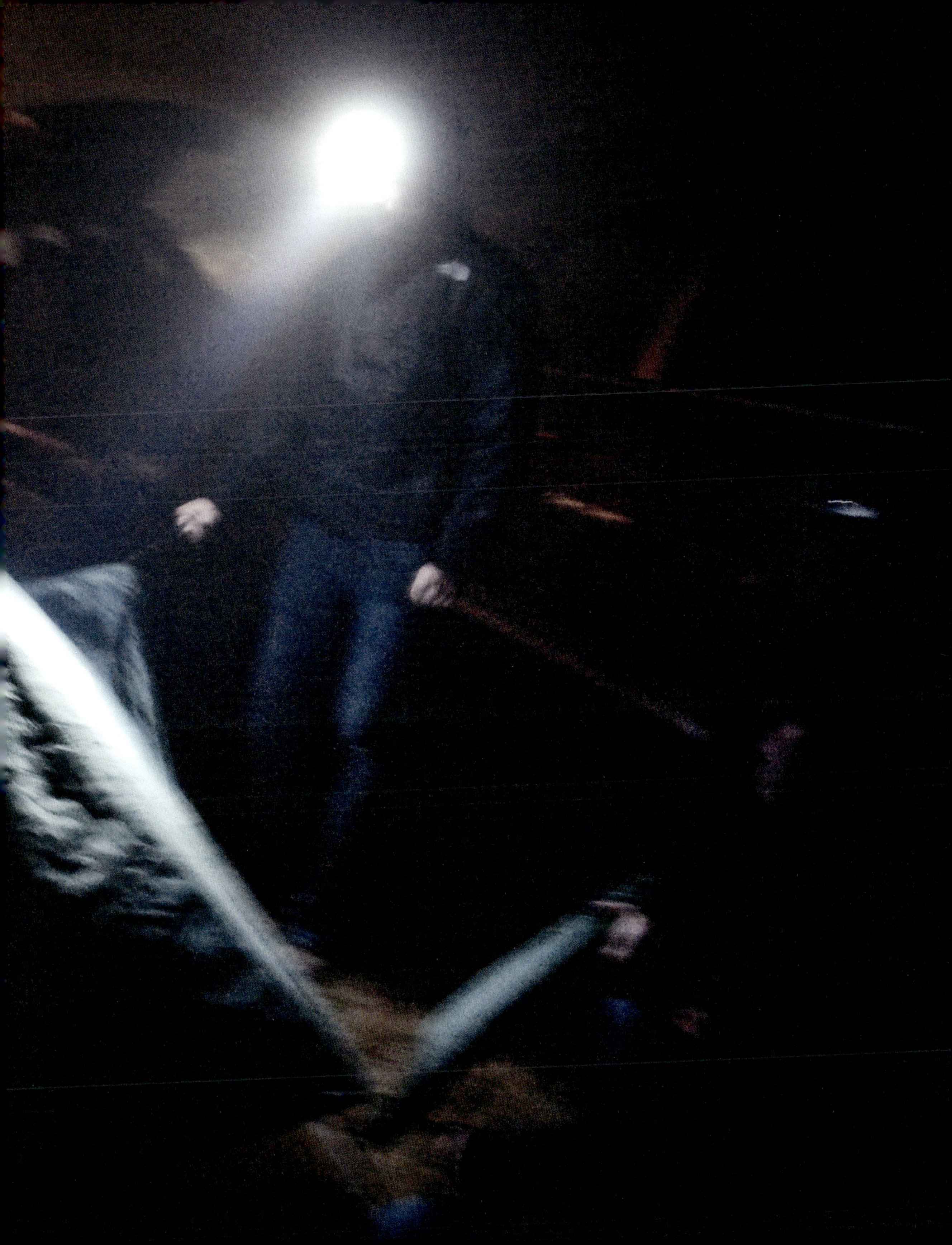

Life Itself Flows Between The Lines

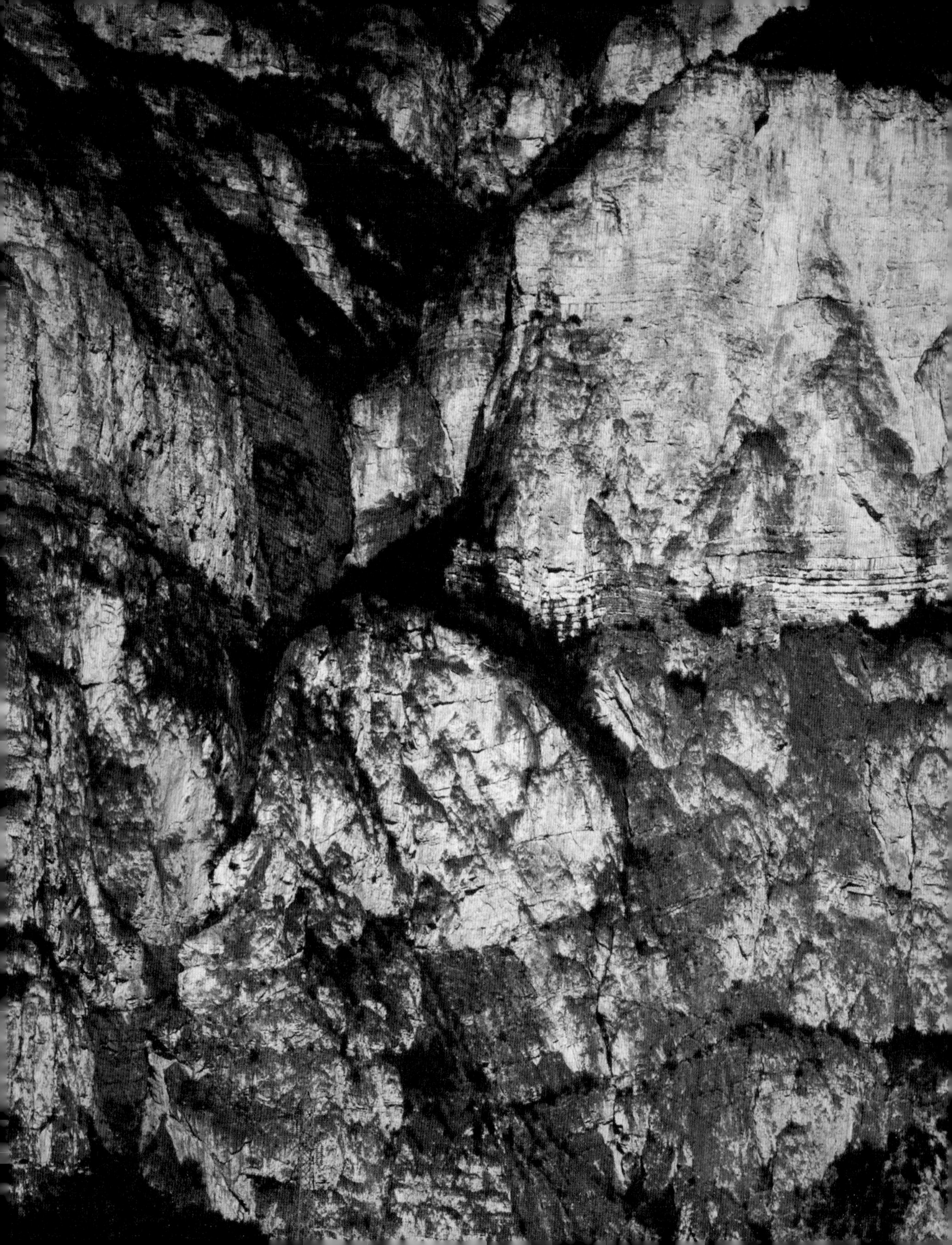

Light and darkness give birth to colour
Day and night, morning and evening create
Morn and evening waking and sleep orchestrate.

Inside and out pose the tension of transition
Zenith and nadir may be said to confer
On each waking man his upright position
Past and future each moment to predicate.

Incarnation and excarnation bring life about
Good and evil to man the truth can teach
Ahriman and Lucifer enable the human spirit
A healthy balance to reach
Between hardening and disintegration
Between sclerosis and inflammation.

Birth and death are sentinels of life
Childhood and old age the frontiers thereof
Joy and sorrow provide our daily bread
But love is the fount of our immortality
O'er boundaries beyond time to eternity –
Love our only humanity.

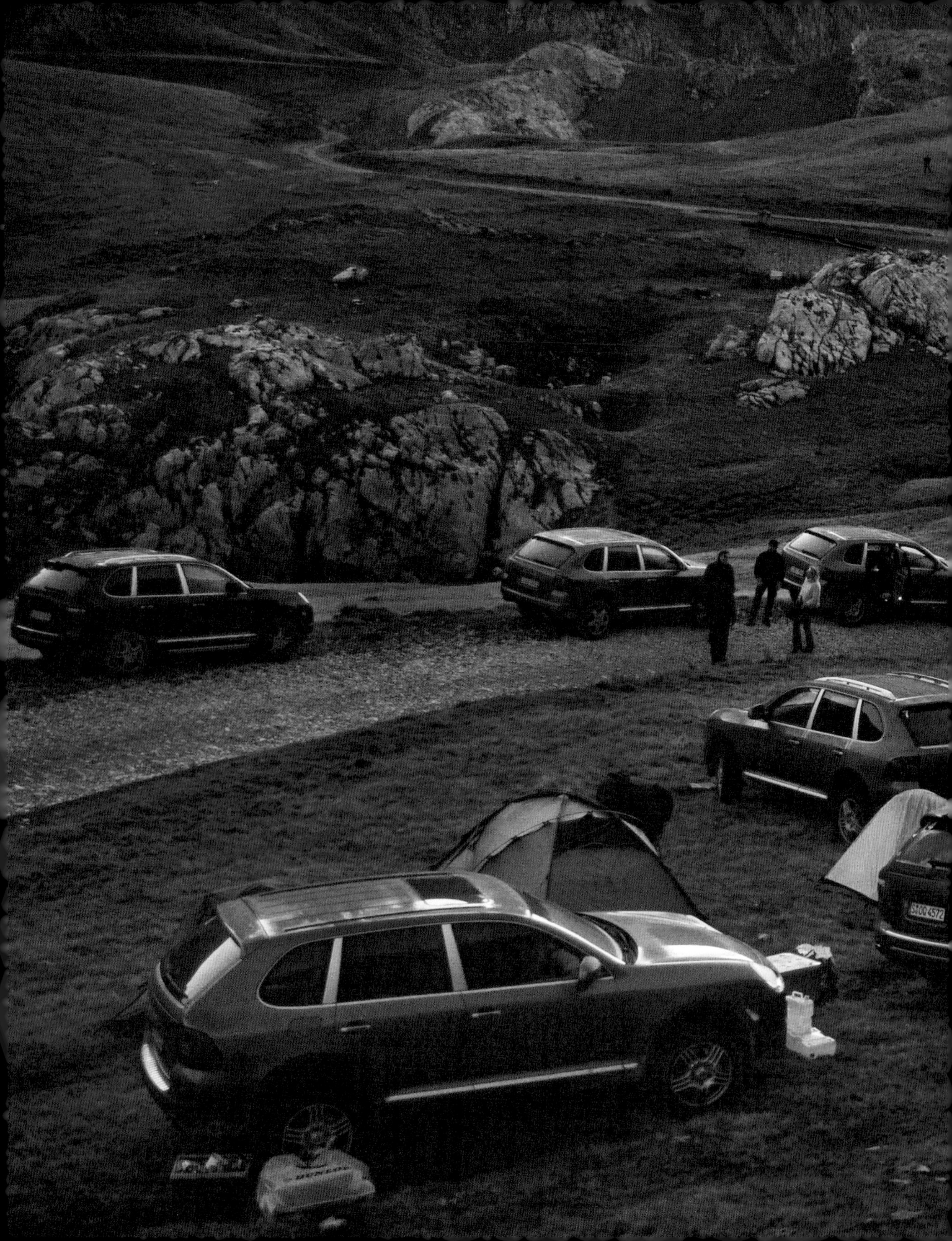

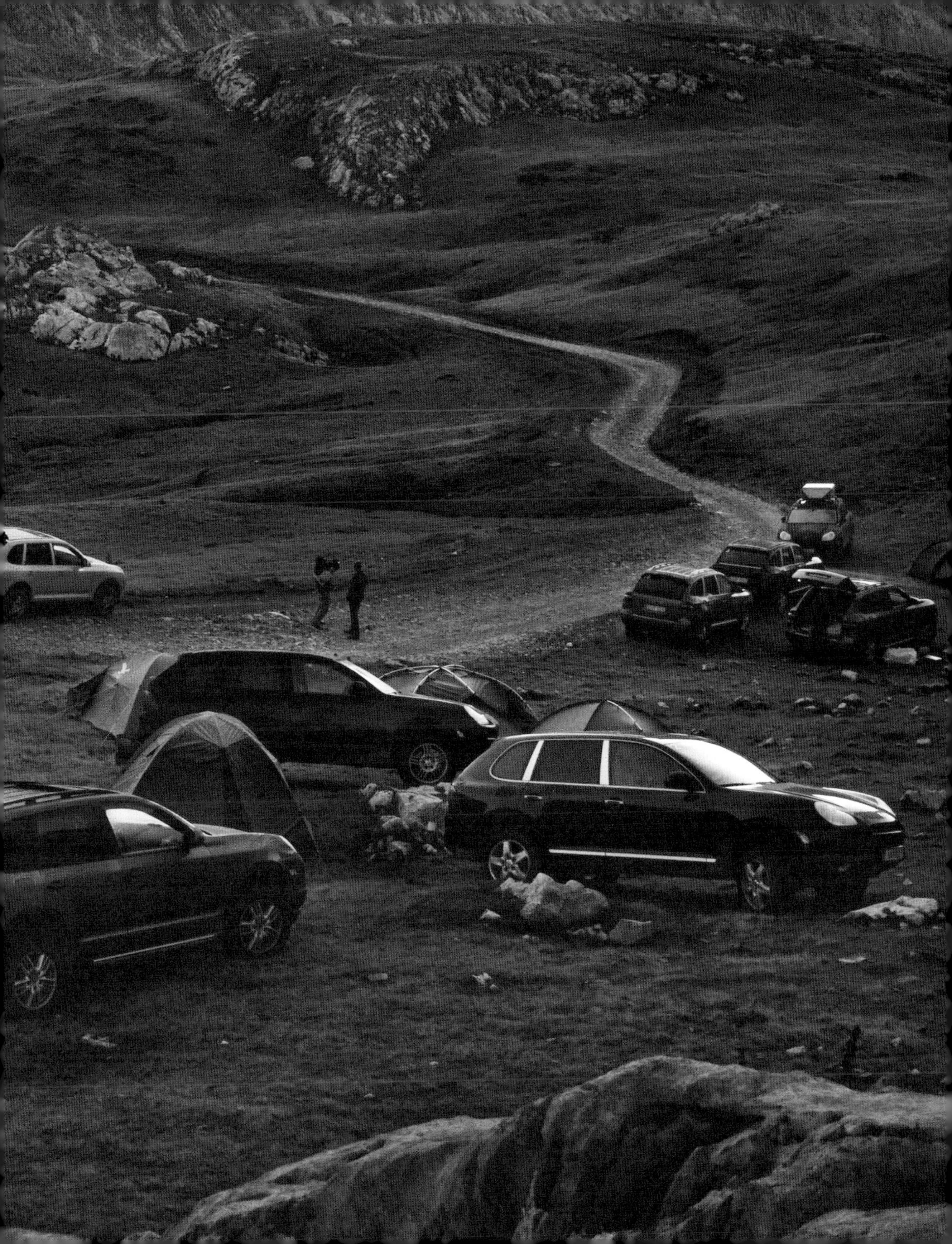

A New-Born Day

In hazy mist
the far valley lies
and o'er the peaks
of stony mass
scintillates –
as the silver chime
of bells long ago
in my home town –
the first shaft of sun
in tremulous
anticipation.

Now emanates
the next beam of sun
like the note of a flute
in that cathedral –
enveloped full
in the organ's swell –
to reverberate
in reverent song
thro' the firmament
and all along
the high peaks.

And then
as once
on Creation's first day
burst forth to soar
out of morning dark
unwavering –
in lambent blaze
and steadfast rays –
the great golden sun.

In countenance
it shone
like eternal youth –
perpetually
rejuvenated –
and each human soul
with caressing smile
it captivated.

Then up rose the mist
and in deference
to the warmth
of this new day
its wisps
evaporated
and slipped away.

Now the countryside
awoke from its sleep
the animal world
and mankind too –
done with dreaming all.
So stillness gave way
to the call of the day,
peace and quiet
giving place
to life's
endeavour –
another pace

into a new day –
and many days to come…!

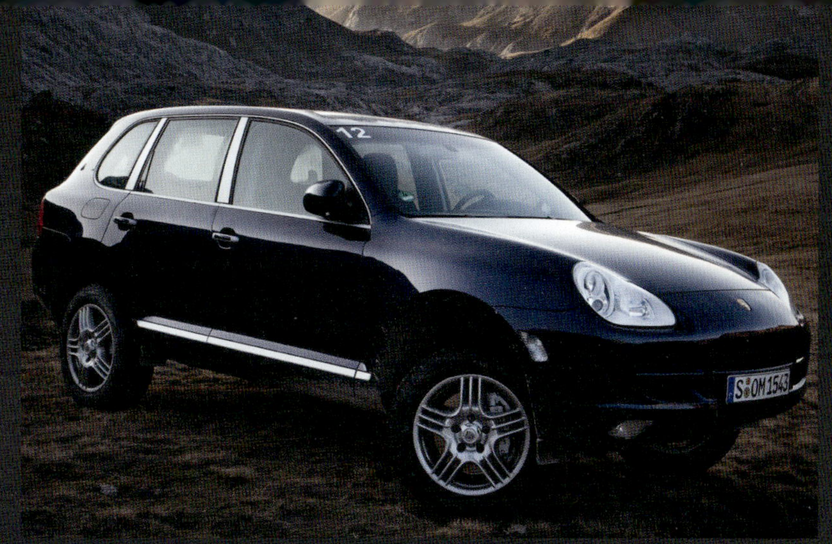
12
S OM 1543

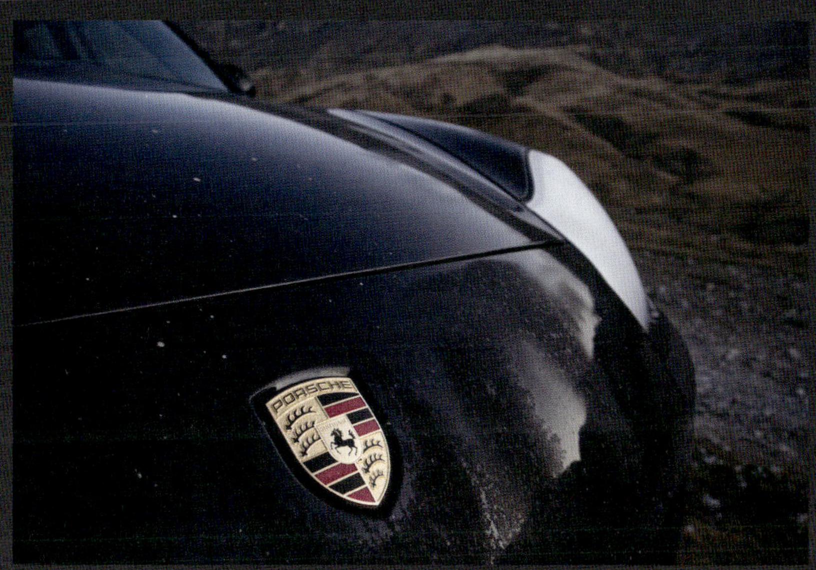
PORSCHE

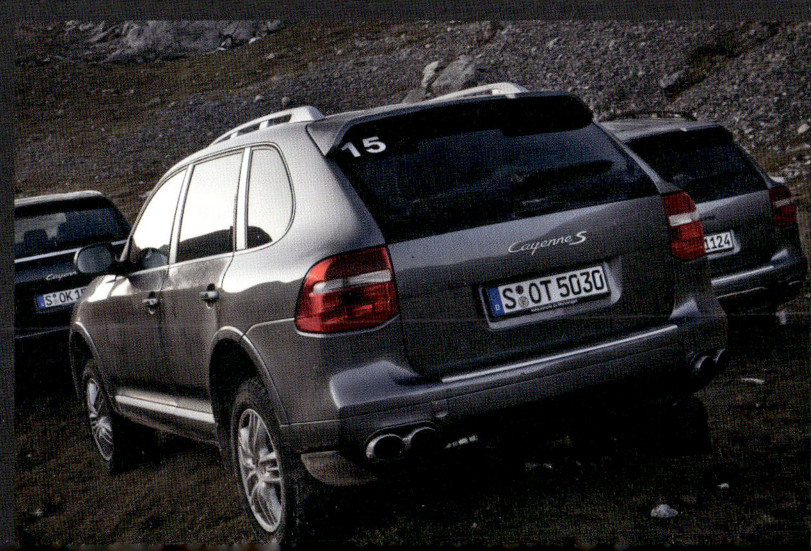
15
Cayenne S
S OT 5030

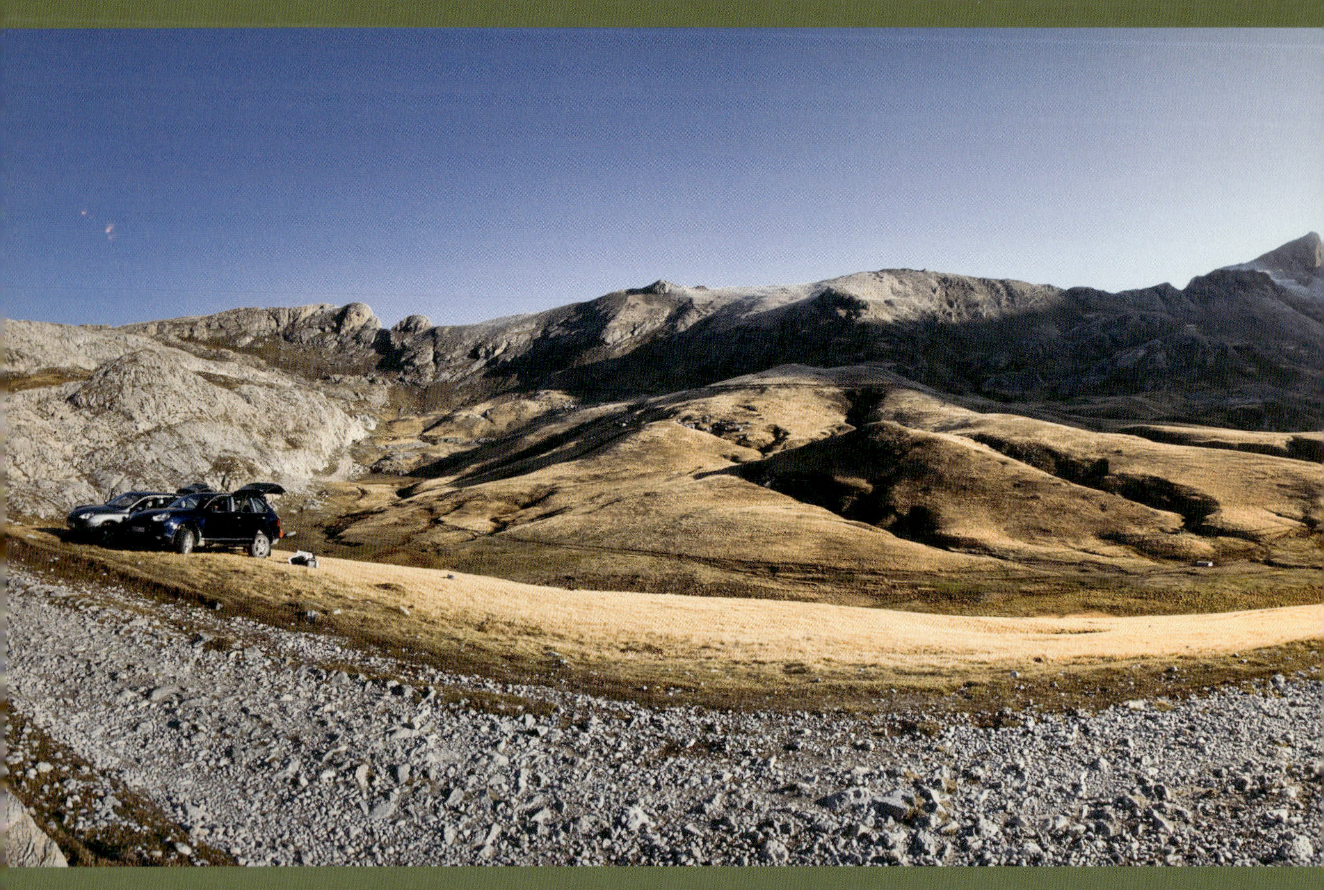

Lotus

At dawn down alongside the water's seam
Swayed Iris in soft mist as in a dream,
As now with the early sun-rays crowned
From every meadow the brooks resound,
Violet-blue she bestowed with her flower
A zest for life in generous shower,
Frond reflections o'er the pearly lake cast,
Dispelled melancholy dreams of the past.

Facing the west the fire-sphere rose higher
And Mother Earth to rejoice did aspire,
Deep to the season's spirit thrilled,
As, bursting from the rain clouds o'er-spilled,
Torrents were unleashed upon the ground,
Iridium in the fire-glow found –
Evening unfolded to herald the night;
From rivers far rose the last gleam of light.

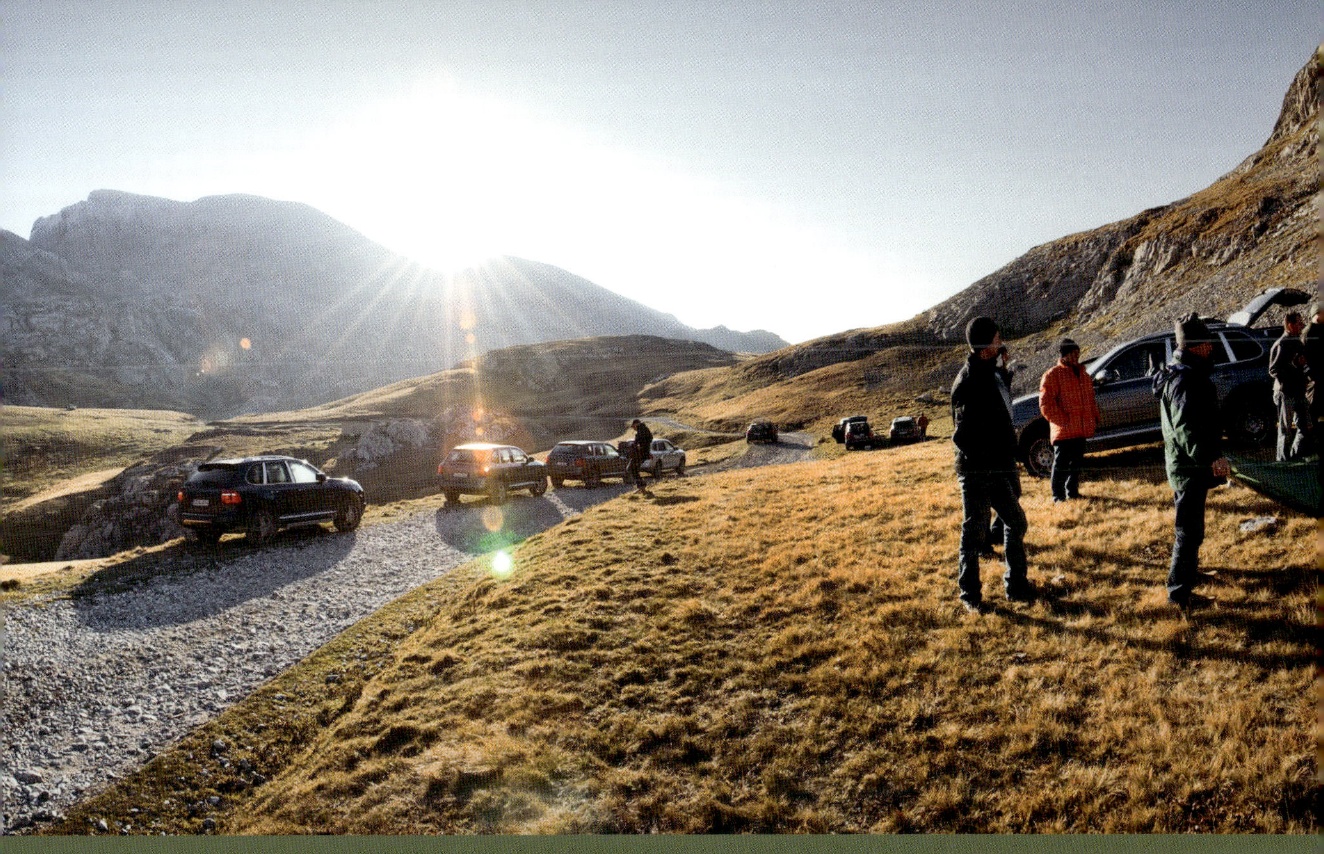

Iridium in dualism failed,
As now the last pangs of sunset exhaled,
Showing by the pale moon's sinister glow
Through mists, dancing and chanting in a row,
Ethereal elves in the dim half-light
And water-nymphs spry on the marshes of night;
While a veil of coldness came down to efface
All the warmth of that familiar place.

Such rites of crystalline diversity
Evoked their myths in icy symmetry,
Evolved each pure geometric token
In consummate metres, from death awoken.
By the shine of stars in the deep midnight
They resolved in harmony to unite,
And Creation's new day to greet with delight –
While winds of spring put the winter to flight.

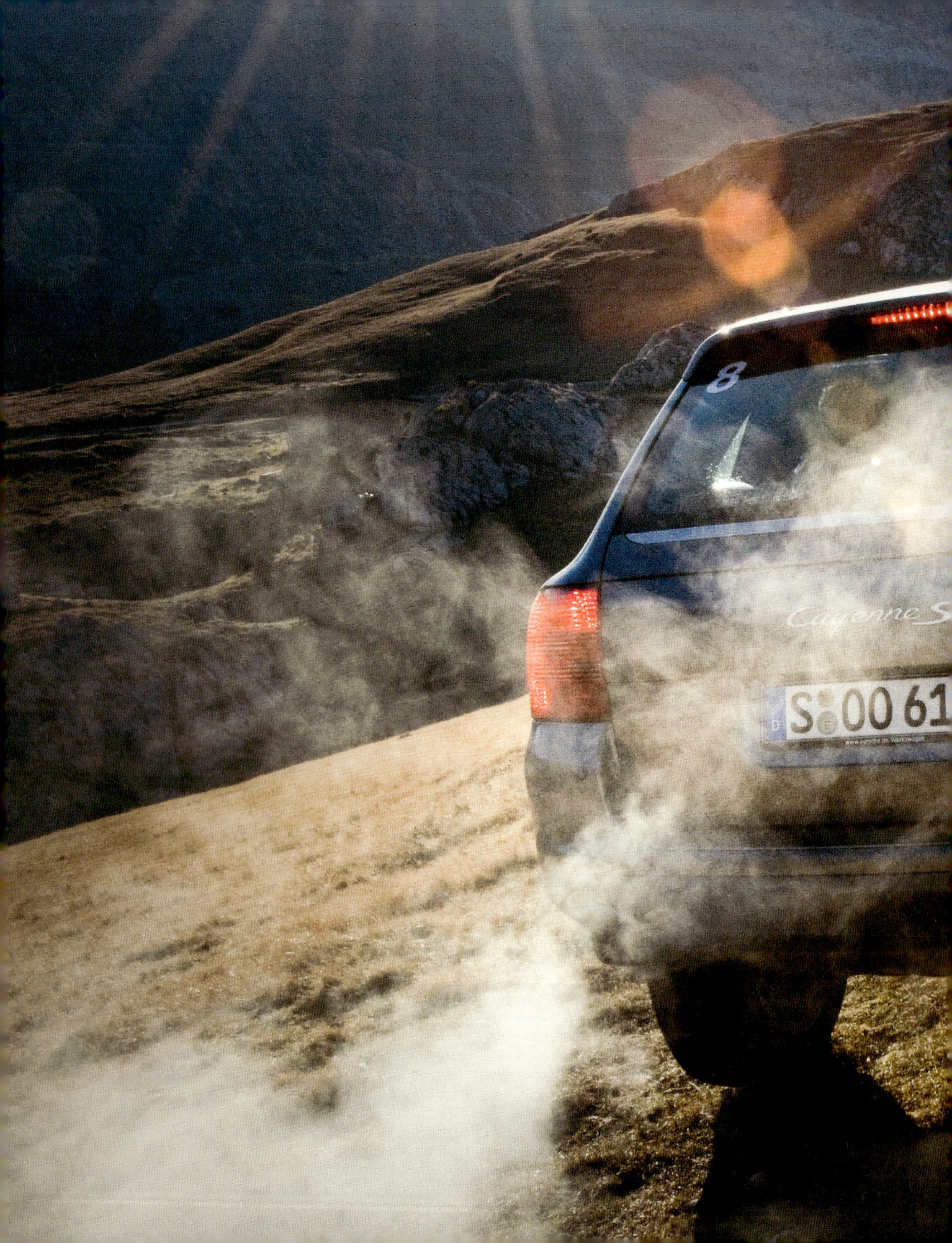
Cayenne S
S 00 61

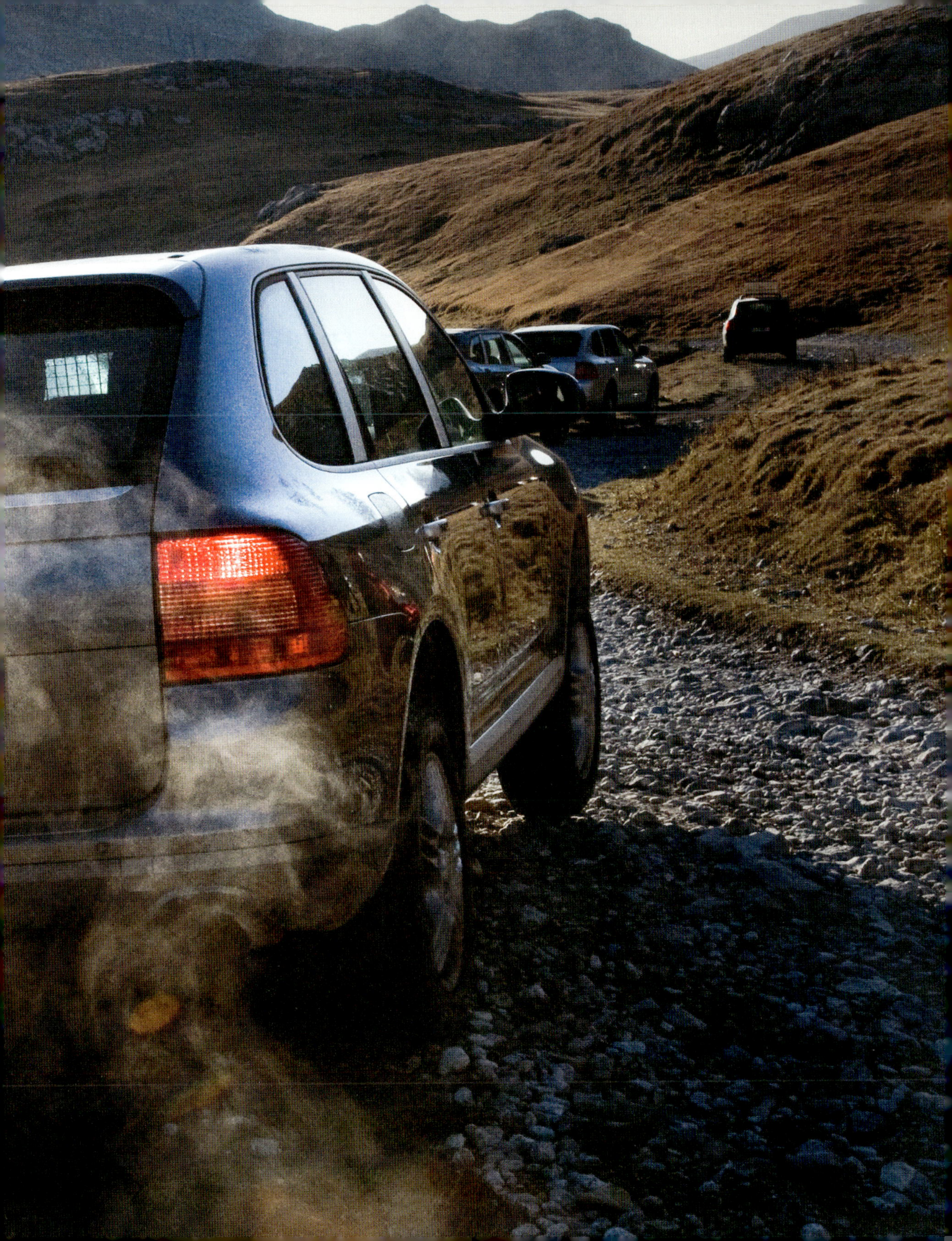

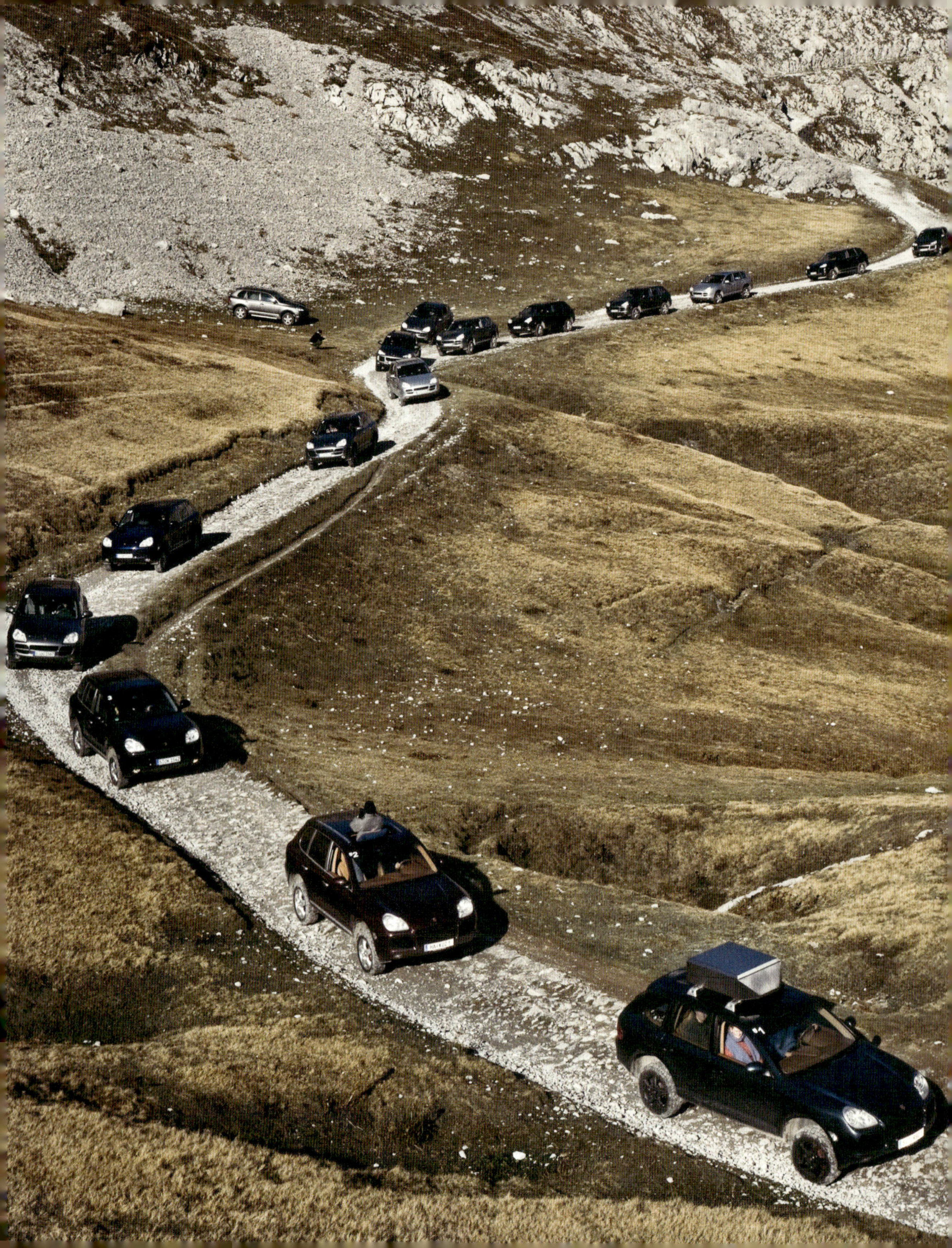

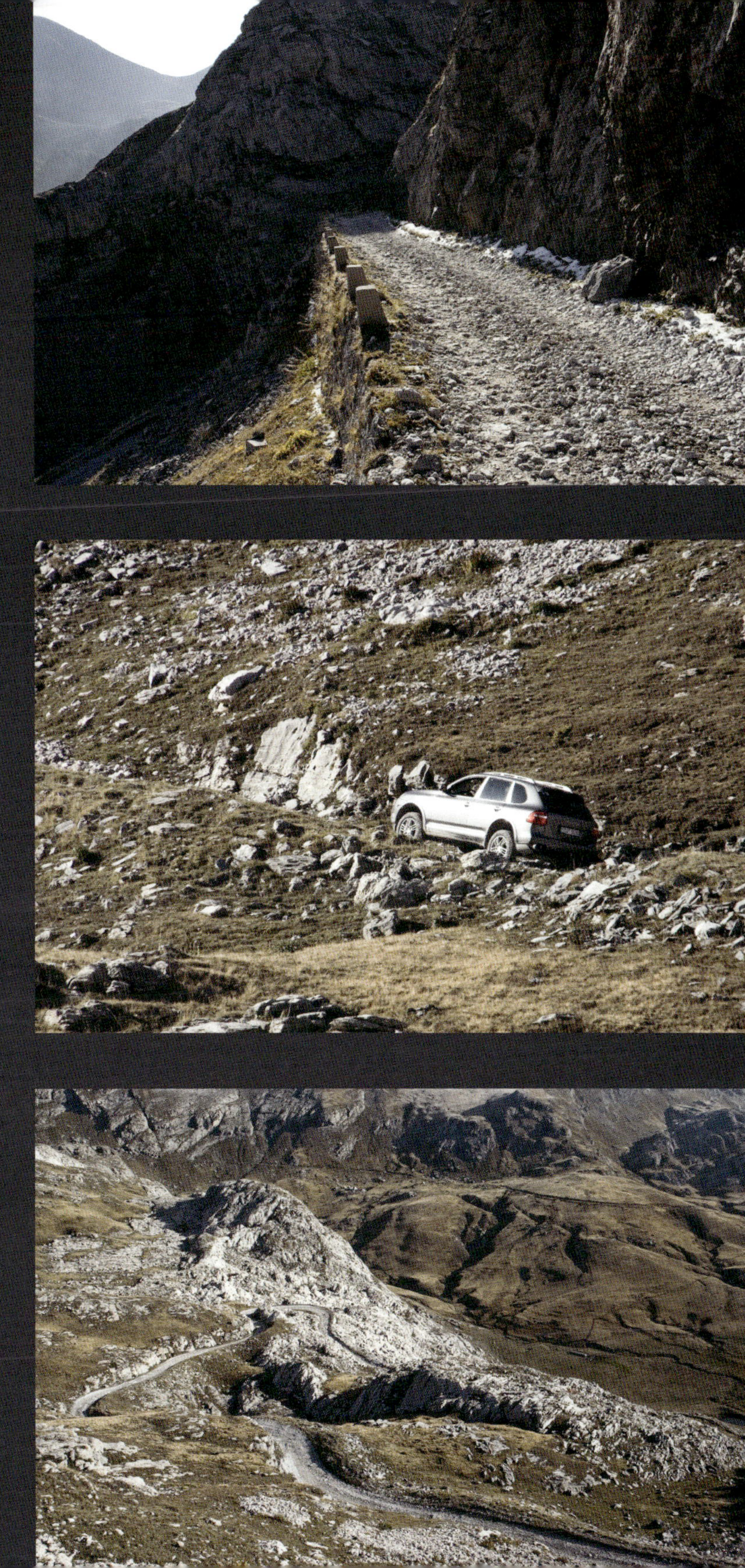

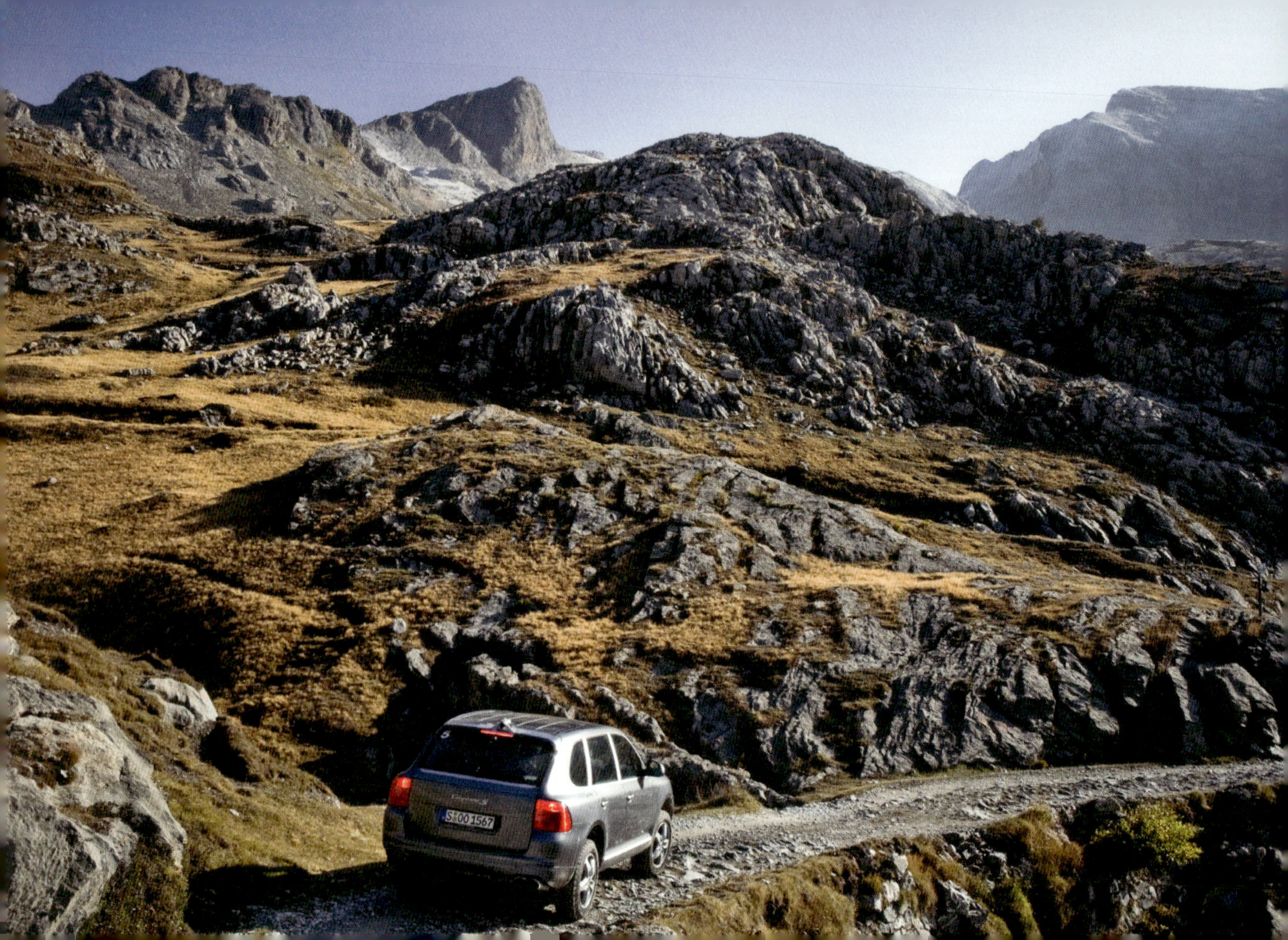
S 00 1567

The Fields Of God

The full moon beamed
To hail the sun,
And mute lay the mist
Inert o'er the rivers,
As black water streamed
Silent down to the Danube.

The skies filled with light
And, the silence defying,
Across the dark fields
All at once rang out
Beyond, clear and bright,
The rush of the river.

The face called God's Rock
Was ablaze and aglow:
A crag of red now –
And from God's field below,
Came new harvests of life.

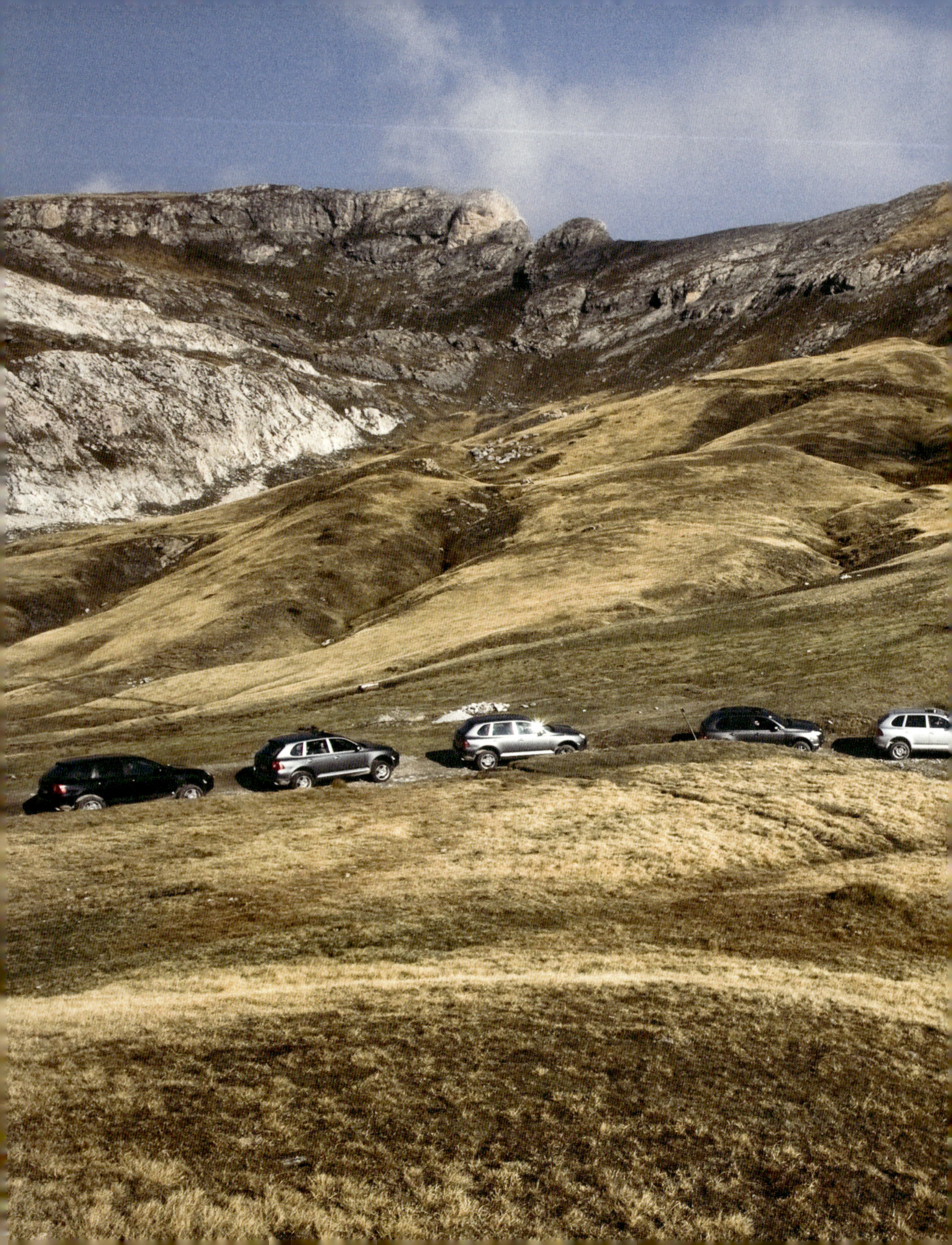

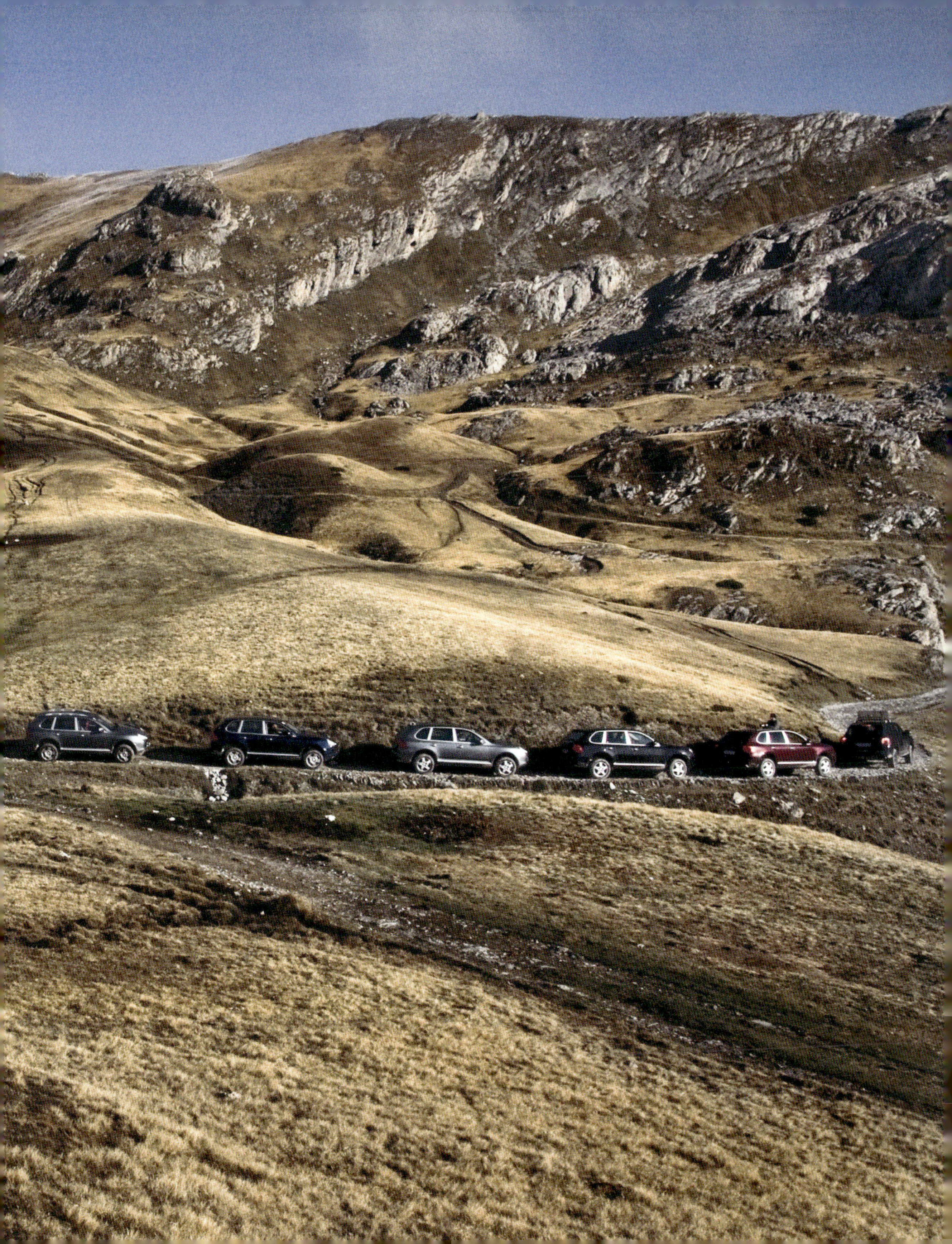

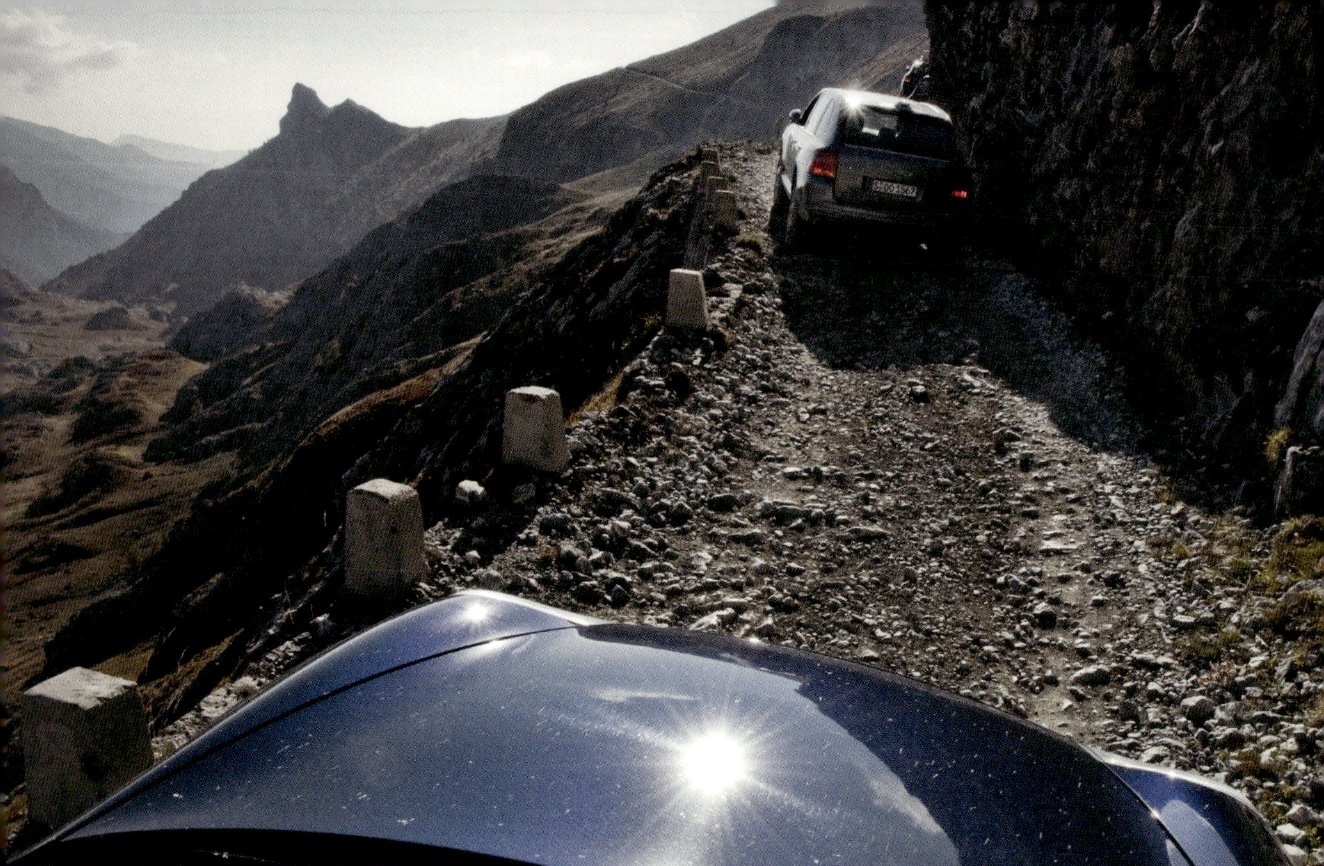

Lonely Abroad

There is a far-off place
Where flows a limpid stream,
Today its course to trace
Remains my fondest dream.

But it is not to be
Whatever I prefer,
It's the barren plain for me:
The lonely traveller.

The road leads on forever,
A stony field to plough,
Alas, I must endeavour
To cross this desert now.

Out on the dreary fen
I've seen fairies dance at night,
But to see you once again
I yearn with all my might.

I'd see your smile so fair
And take you by the hand,
If I could just be there
At home in my own land.

But I must travel on
And leave this place today,
No more the fairies' song:
They all have flown away.

No matter where I go,
It is a foreign place,
The only sight I long for
Is your delightful face.

It is not mine to say
If ever I'll return,
Or here abroad must stay,
And heavy-hearted yearn.

And so I persevere,
Others' paths I must pursue,
But wish my dearest dear
A fond good-night to you!

May God watch o'er my sleep
And save me from dark powers
That sinister vigils keep
And round the hawthorn lower.

But should my dreams come true
And we meet again, my heart,
For my life I promise you,
We never more shall part!

No longer can I stay
Where these clear waters flow,
God's blessing now I pray,
As lonely on I go.

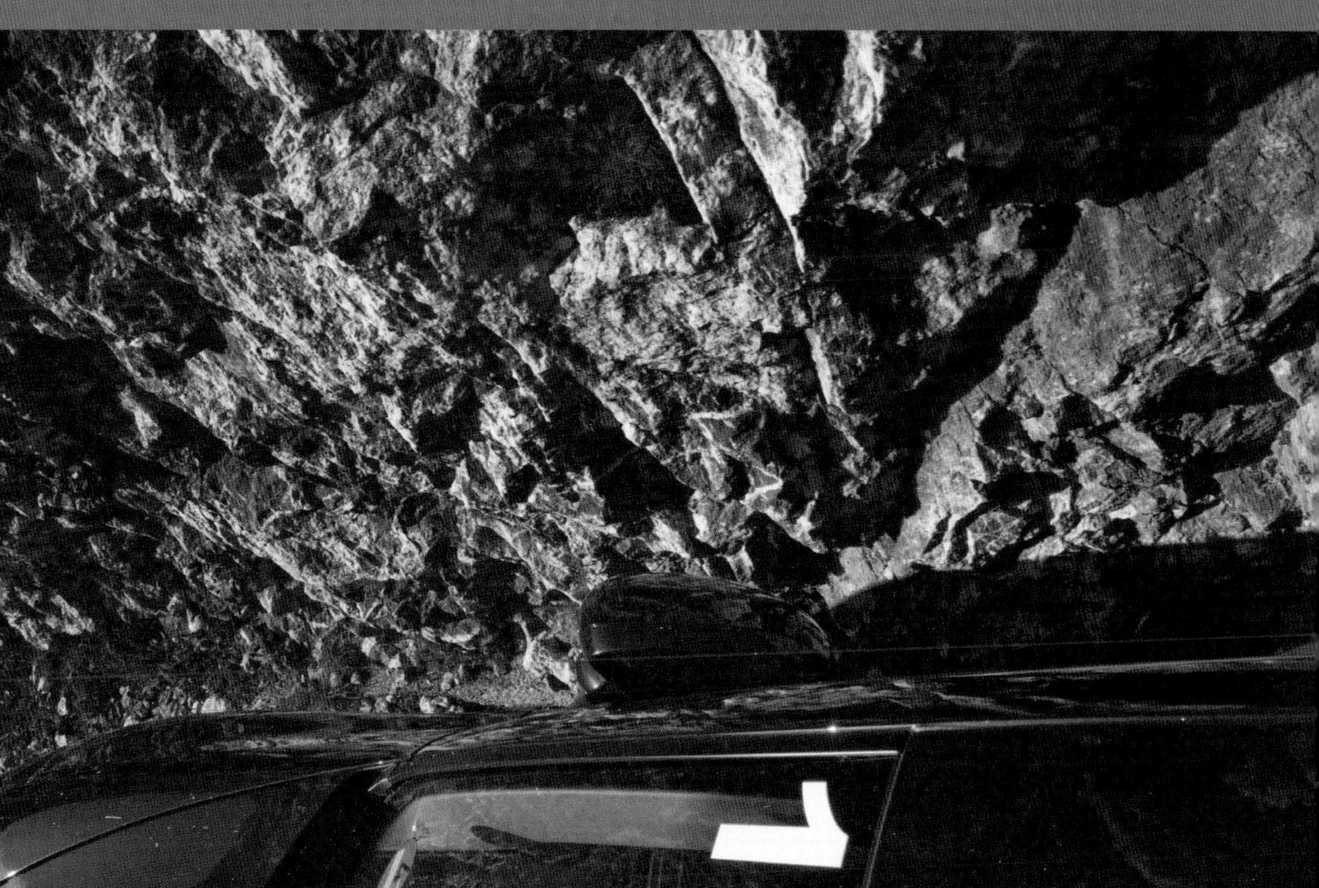

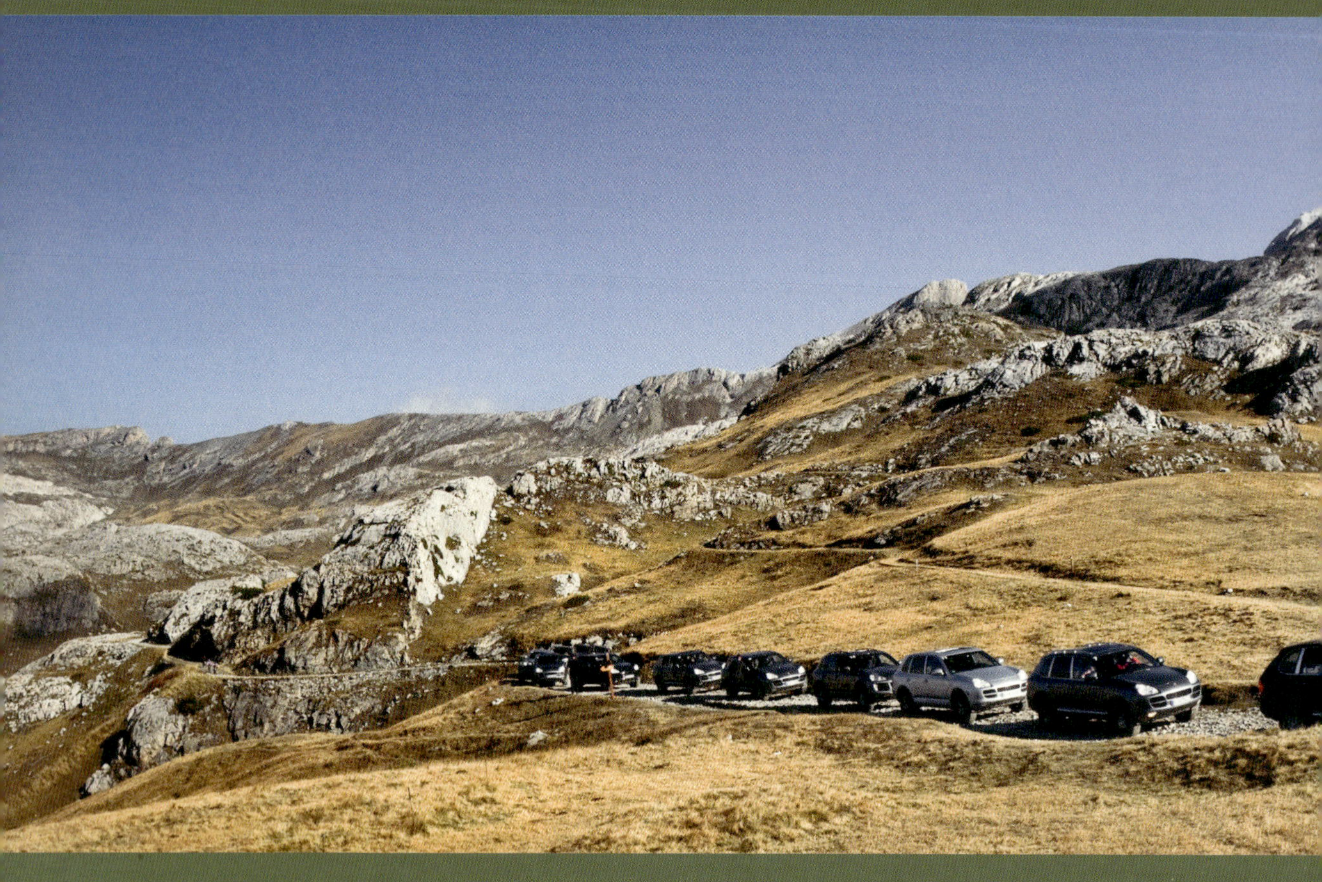

Autumn's Hour

And now all the world turns to grey,
All bare are the pastures and trees –
As southwards the birds fly away
Leaving fields still as lifeless seas.

The storm wind swirls under the eaves,
The rain 'gainst the windows to sweep –
It seems like the wail of banshees
Awoken from summer's long sleep.

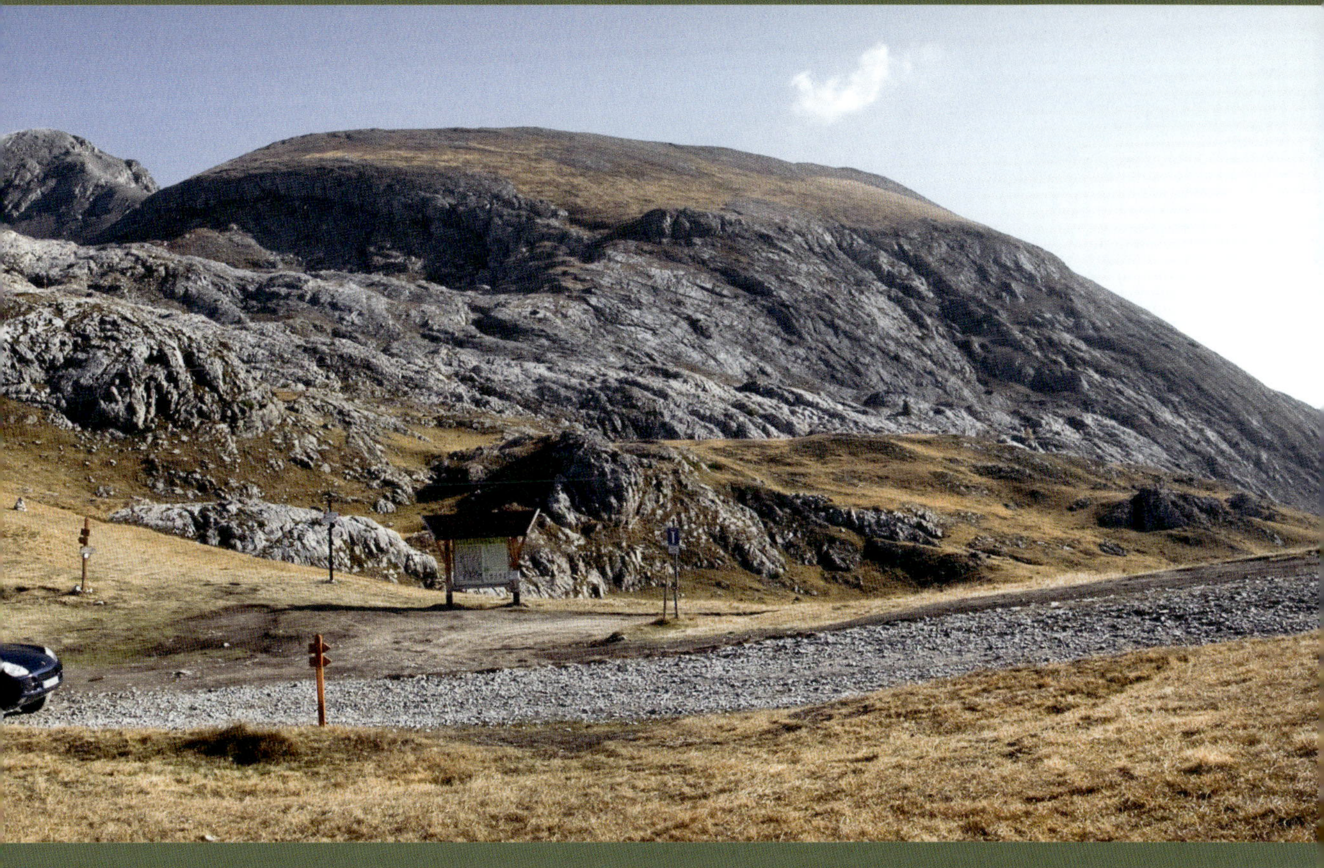

Yet from such stormy life's air
The song that we seem to hear,
Is that this death in Autumn's hour
By the wind is cherished most dear.

It's an ill wind that blows no good
With its ever-enlivening breath –
So the air whirls round as it should
Stirring up new life out of death.

Lonely Paths

The going is hard now where it once was easy
As hand in hand we used to make our way –
Alas, the time came for that love to leave me
How hard it is for us when skies are grey!

How difficult we find it as we strive
To hear the voice of love, it is so rare –
How hard it is to keep that song alive
So that some day we once again may care.

But since the magic word I used to know –
It rings through me when hours and days are bright,
And carries me away from here below
To the farthest star of ethereal night:

So in my very heart this word I keep,
And for that by-gone sorrow no more weep.

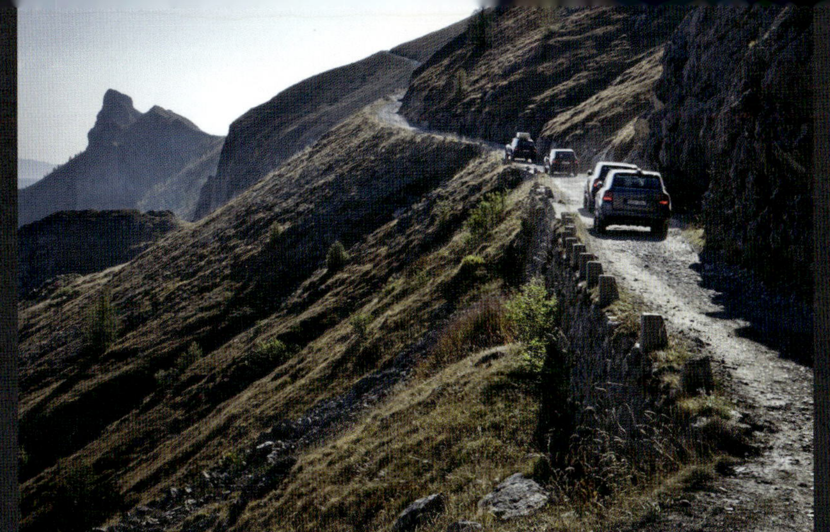

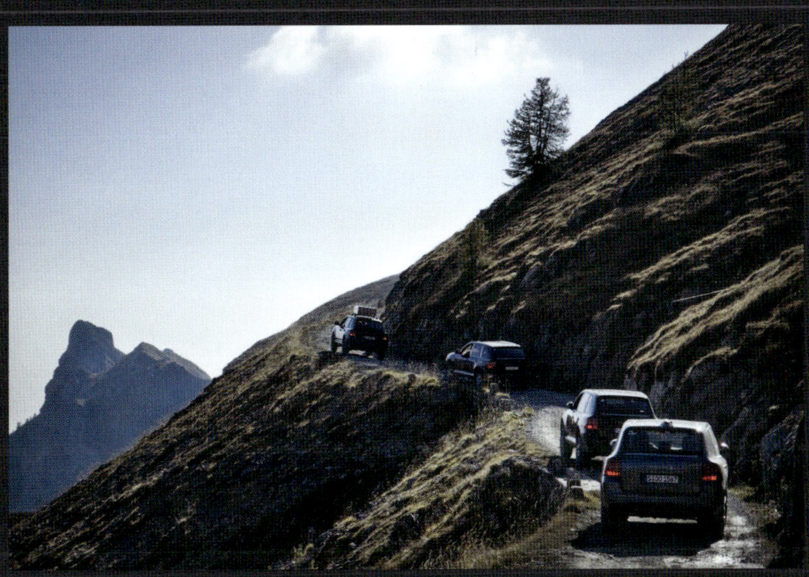

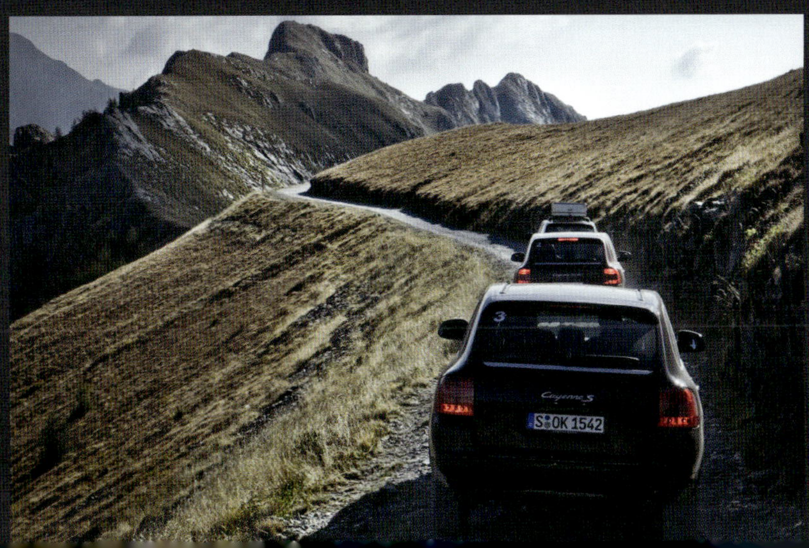
S OK 1542

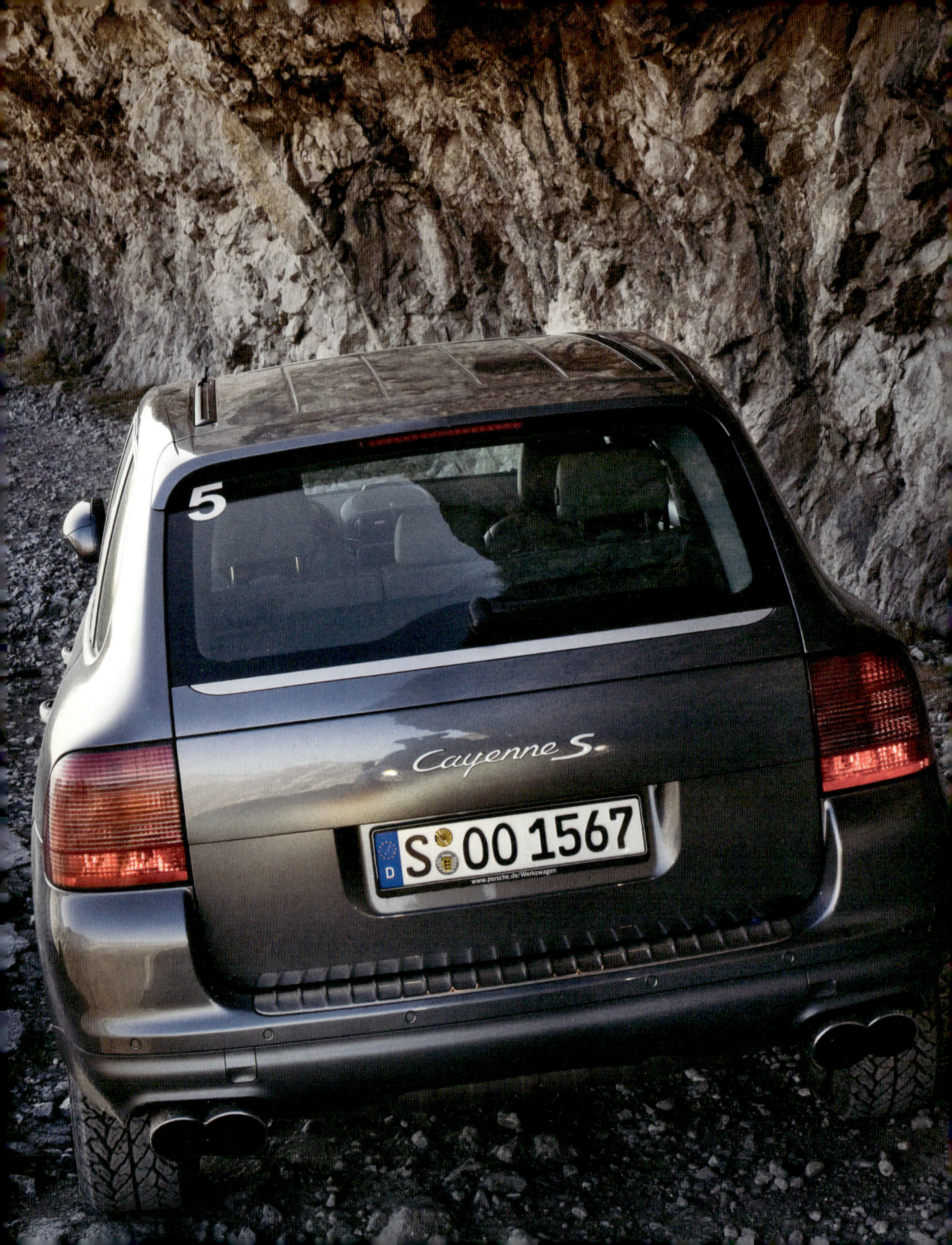
5
Cayenne S
S 00 1567
www.porsche.de/Werkswagen

Searching

A man sets out on a journey,
The ice cracks all around,
He seeks the warmth of company –
But none is to be found.

He searches for the meaning of life,
Yet a mystery it remains,
He longs to rise above mortal strife –
But all in vain.

He tries to resist death's icy sway,
But soon begins to waver,
Far and wide finding only disdain –
And not his Saviour.

Laid low and the worse for wear,
No mercy did he implore –
Ice-cold he died, on his lips a prayer,
And then the light he saw.

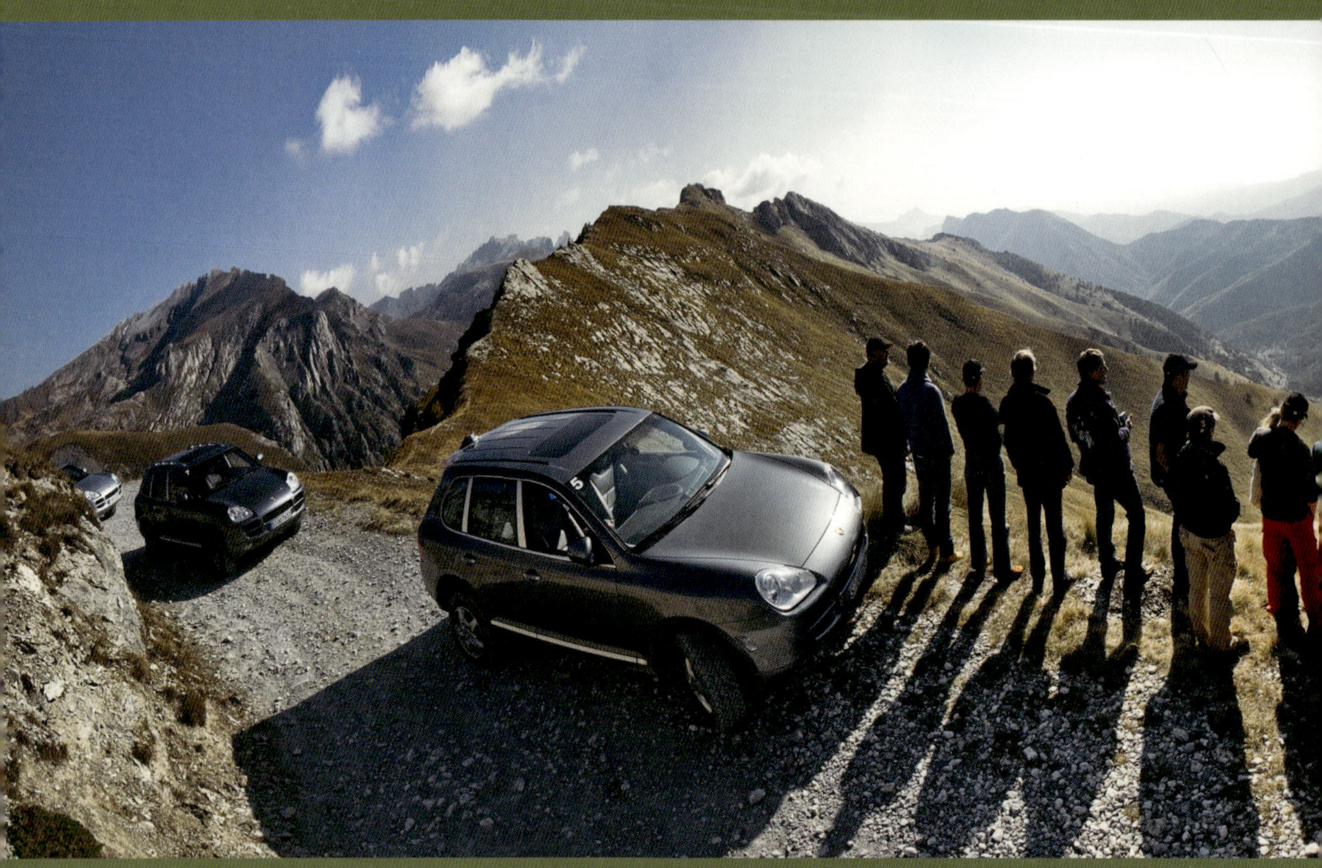

An Eagle

An eagle,
I wish I were
an eagle,
yes –
inscrutable

as a ruler
holding sway
over all worlds,
beasts, plants
and men,

above
all distress,
over rock and stone,
in a void,
timeless as

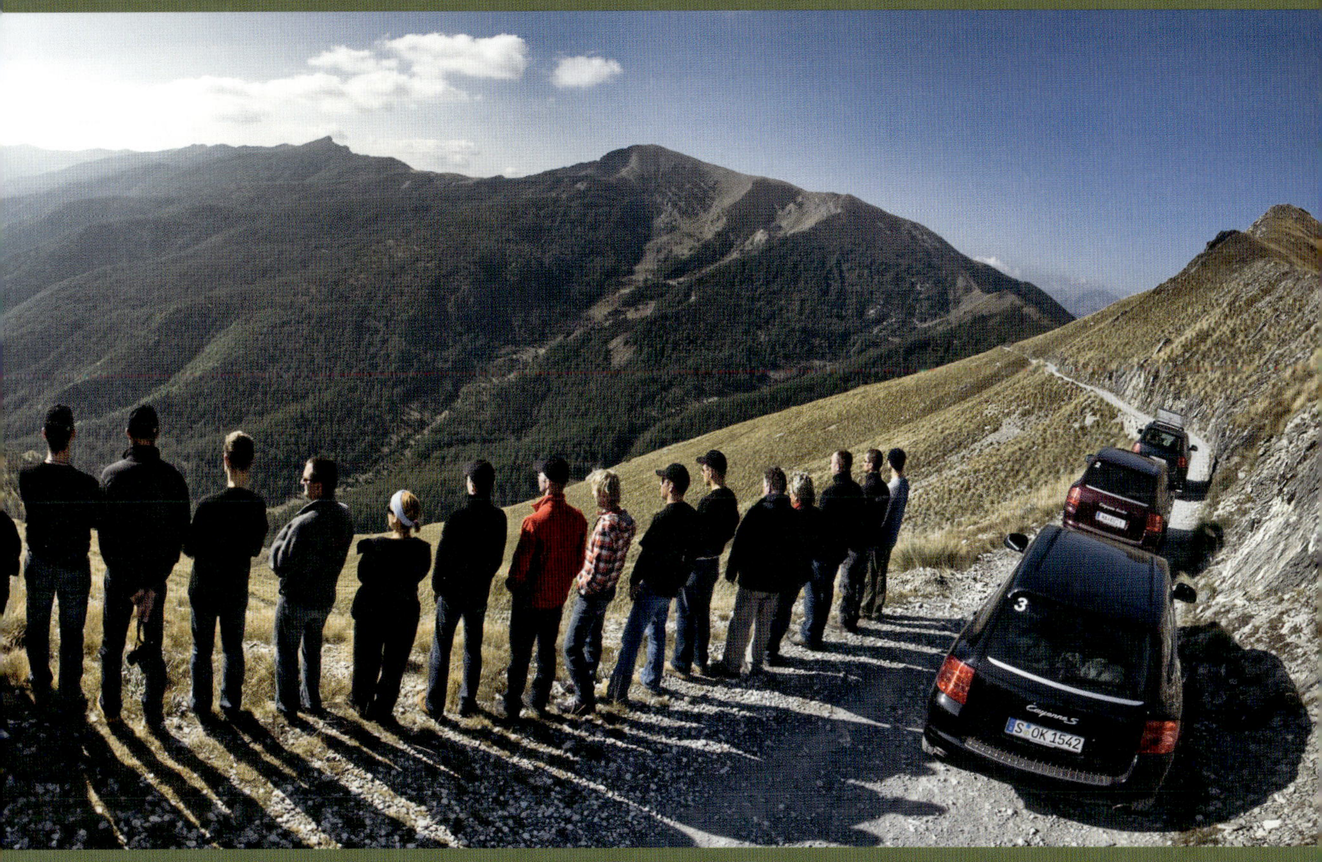

a chimera
hovering aloft
over glaciers
soaring
wide

and away
above
a thousand lands
to the myriads
stars…

An eagle,
were I only
an eagle
ah,
but I am
man!

Away To The Horizon

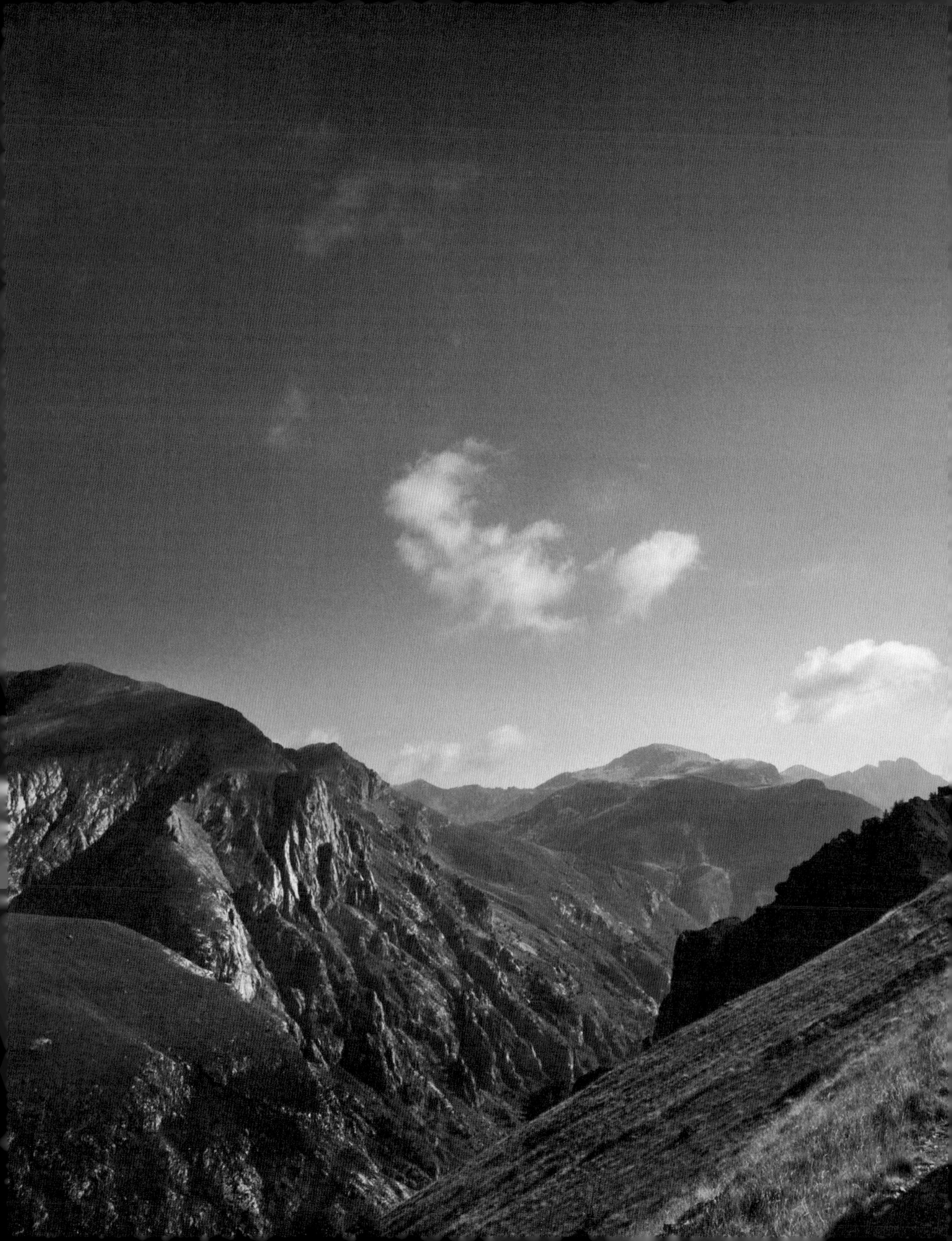

Far o'er distant peaks, away to the horizon
for one last time we gaze upon
that rugged elemental range,
before winding down along a mossy way
thro' meadows soft and humid, with rivulets agleam.
Here now our tired hands we bathe
in a cool and limpid stream.
Then, quenched our thirst, we follow where the river leads:
down the gentle valley
among fragrant chestnut trees.
Now a milder air is wafing from the sea
and from deep gullies waterfalls
are heard to splash and spray.
A rainbow radiates and sparkles in the sun
and the wine-grower's art soon comes into sight,
with his vineyards criss-crossing the warm hillside.
A glimpse of the sea now draws us on down
past a blueness of lake
with its water's black ground,
till we see the first flash and hear the shrill sound
of seagulls in flight.
A sharp horizon stretching to infinity
draws a line between our world and Godly doings.
Only we hold that picture in our memory.
And as the big red sun goes down in that wide sea
we cannot but wonder
how significant are we –
driven by joys and sorrows, our whole life through –
wonder at how the water's cycle lifts it from the sea
to burst from the sky in thunder and lightening hurled,
in torrents of rain once more
to fall upon the world,
then in rivulet and running stream flow back to the sea,
from whence again it rises into the heaven's blue.
So it is with the life of men –
between birth and death and life again.
Only our awareness reaches out night and day
and in the life beyond, the horizon to create…
ever coming and going in time's flowing stream.

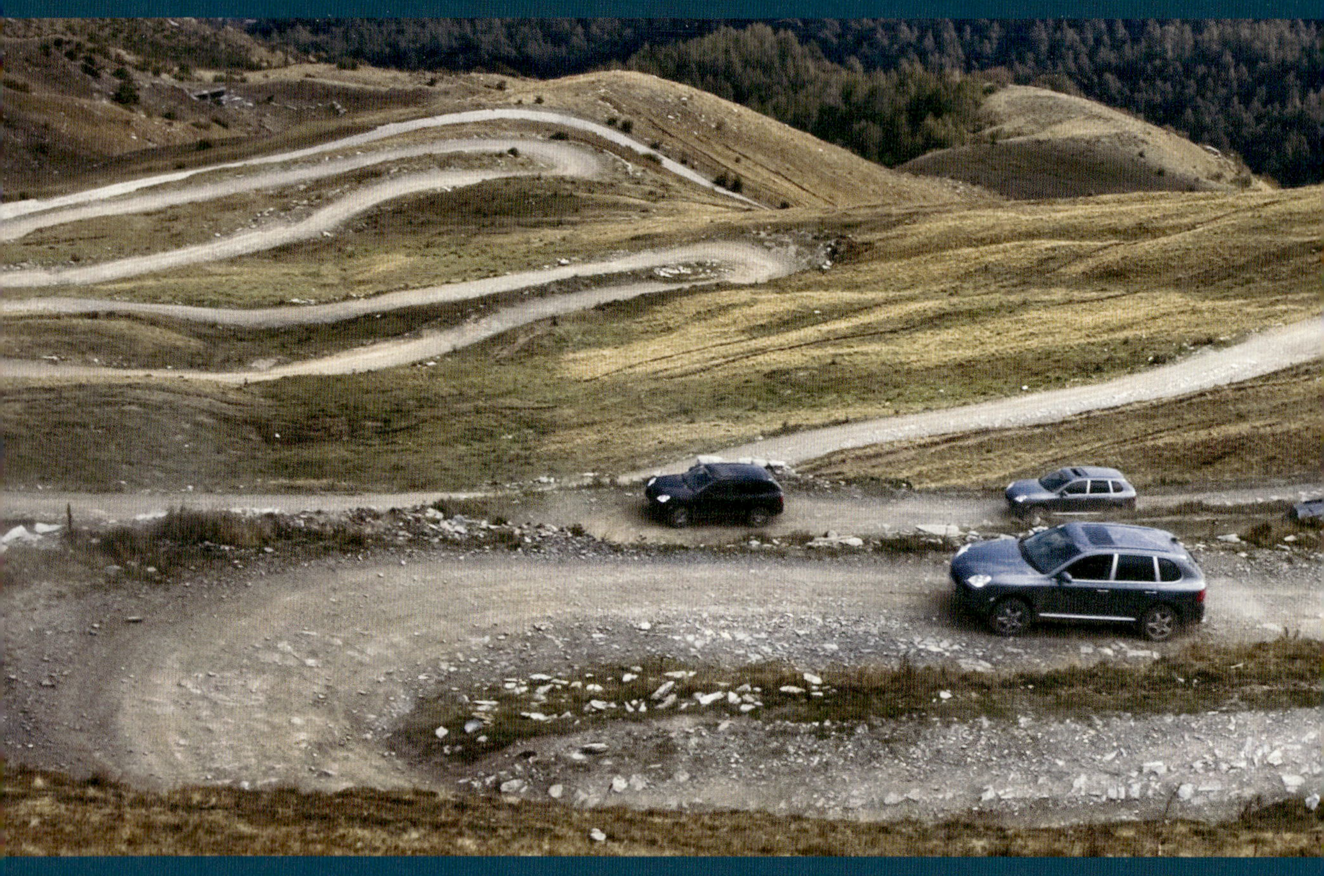

Life is made up of highs and lows and the art of it is to look on the downward turns as opportunity and the upward turns with enthusiasm.

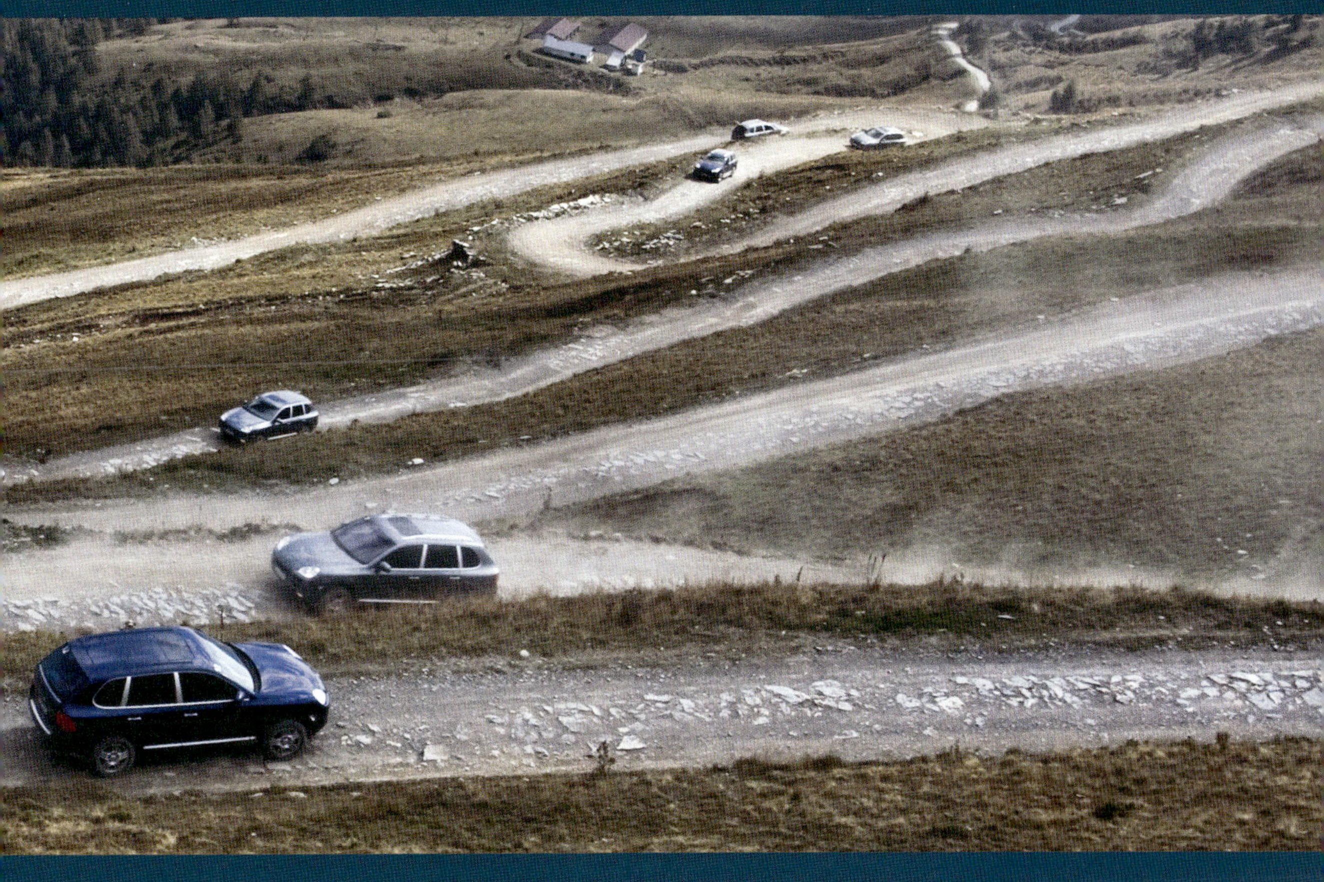

It is not important when and how one reaches one's goal, but essential to have one and then pursue it.

Return

May the soul divine the worlds,
And light kindle mankind;
May wisdom ripen the spirit
And justice fill the mind.

May hope pervade each breath,
And reason claim the voice;
May clarity reign in speech
And love in gain rejoice.

May the future uphold duality,
And night guard our unity;
May tomorrow enfold the new
And the old harbour safely.

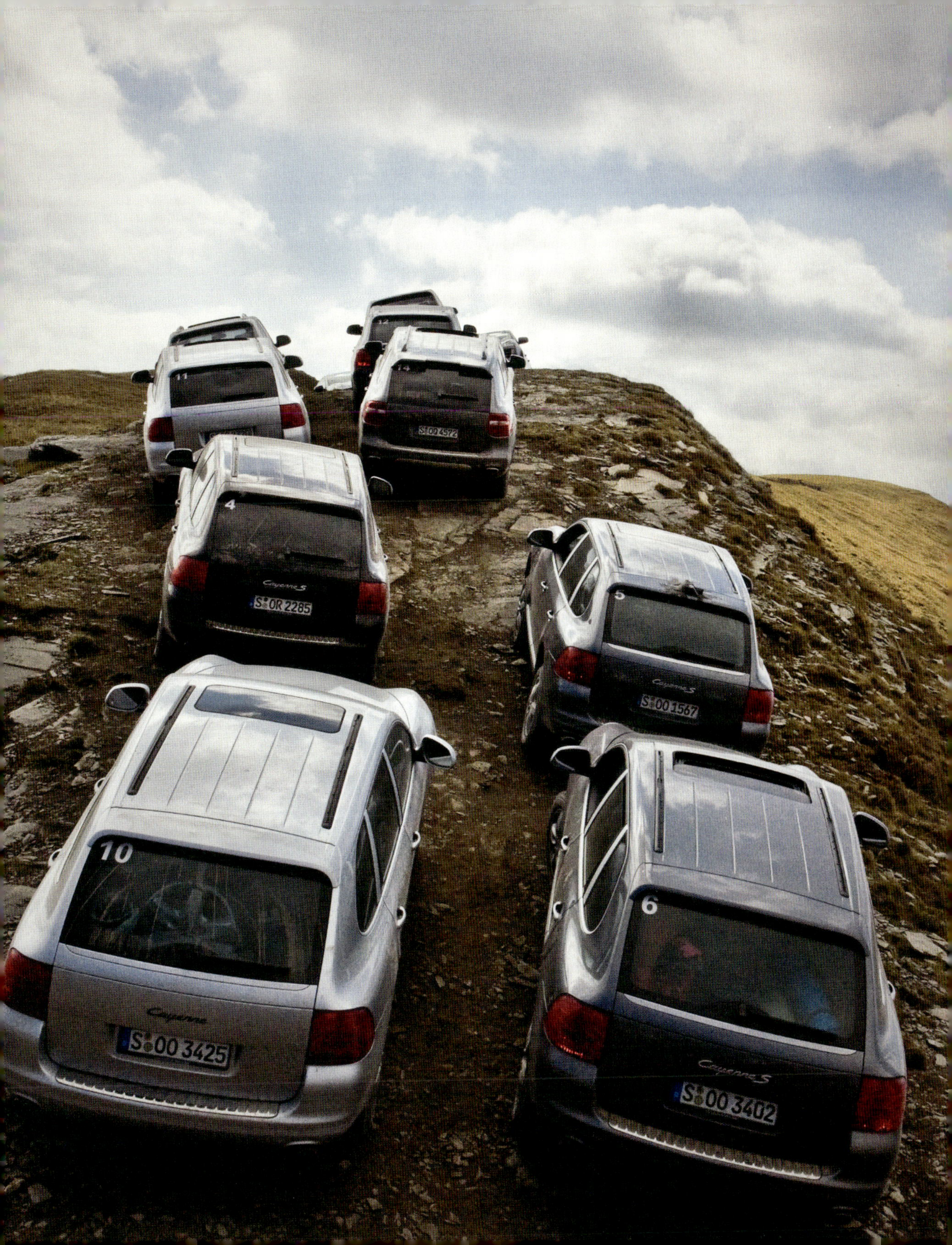
10
S OO 3425
Cayenne
6
S OO 3402
Cayenne S
4
S OR 2285
Cayenne S
S OO 1567
Cayenne S
S OO 4572

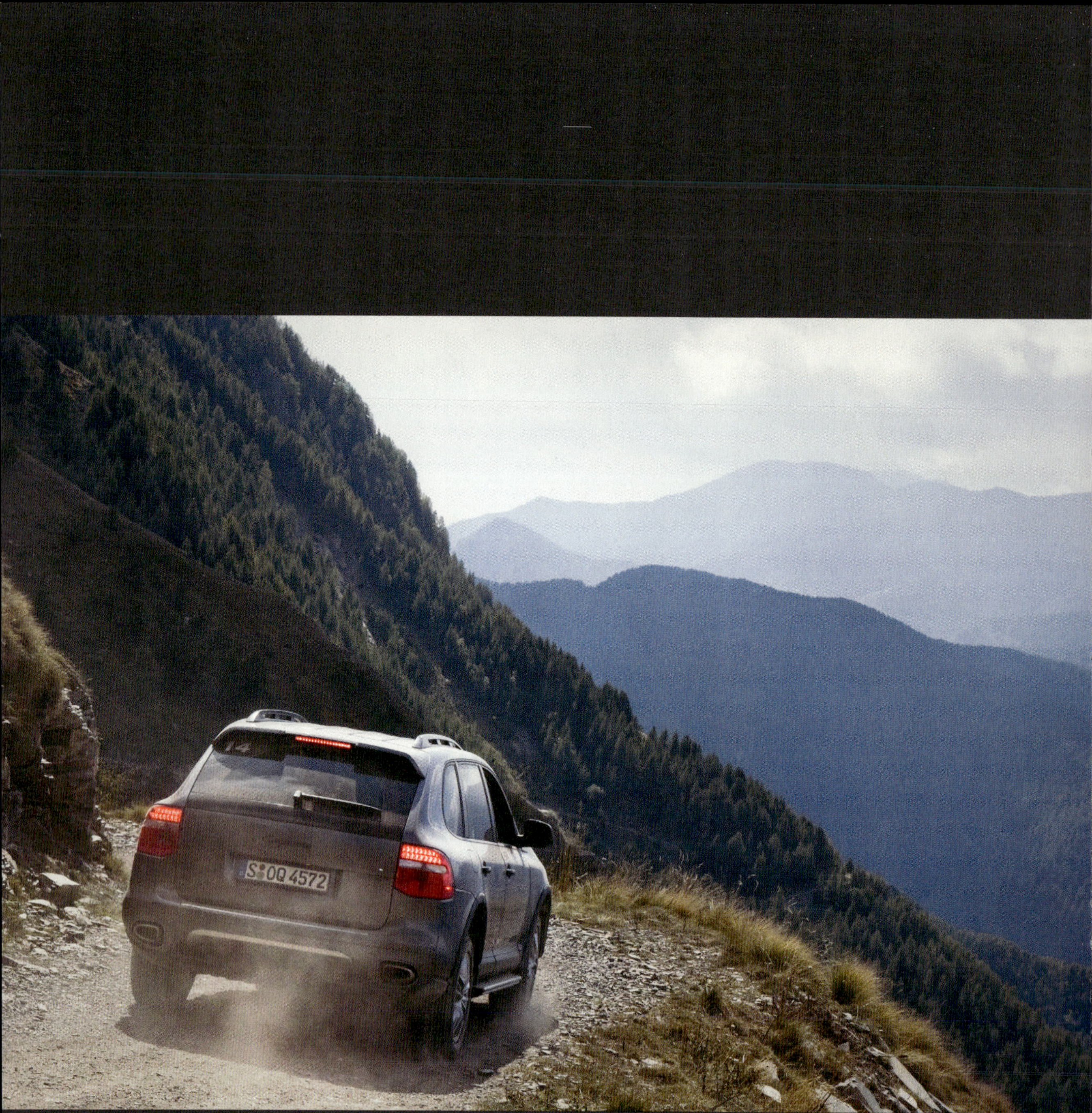
S OQ 4572

Holy Night

Thus again the stilly time draws near –
The worlds in their splendour repose
And love from the blue of night bestows
Hope of thoughtful cheer.

Thus waning is the gloom tonight –
Vanished all trace of dark powers,
New light is born, aspiration flowers
To meet day's challenges aright.

Thus yearning sadness is effaced –
New courage brings serenity
To hearts in strains of joy embraced.

Thus the dream blends with reality –
And unity on the truth is based
'Round the universal Christmas tree.

Cathedral

Black was the beechwood,
The full moon shone out
On that night journey,
Shadows shifted about
At my side so eerie
As if to hail me
In ghostly mockery.

Somewhere close a branch broke
In the breathless glade
But never a voice spoke,
Nor was human sound
My ear to assail
On this night profound –
nor yet nightingale.

A shriek shrilled quite near,
Stars glittered away –
What came over me
I could hardly say –
But the moon's chill shine
Sent a stab of fear
Coldly down my spine.

In the moon-white light
Between the trees
A cross came into sight,
A tower and buttress high…
What on earth could it mean?
Then right before my eyes
A second darting gleam.

It was a cold, dark night
And a stillness lay
Somehow delusively,
O'er ancient masonry
Turrets, ramparts so high –
It seemed that they aspired
To reach out for the sky.

And I no longer knew
The time nor yet the place,
What was false, what true
Of the visions seen –
When lo! A funeral train
Vanished through the mist.
Could it perhaps mean…?

The time moved on at last,
I heard the distant chimes –
So midnight has passed!
It is over, can it be?
Now the new day dawns grey…
Am I really free?

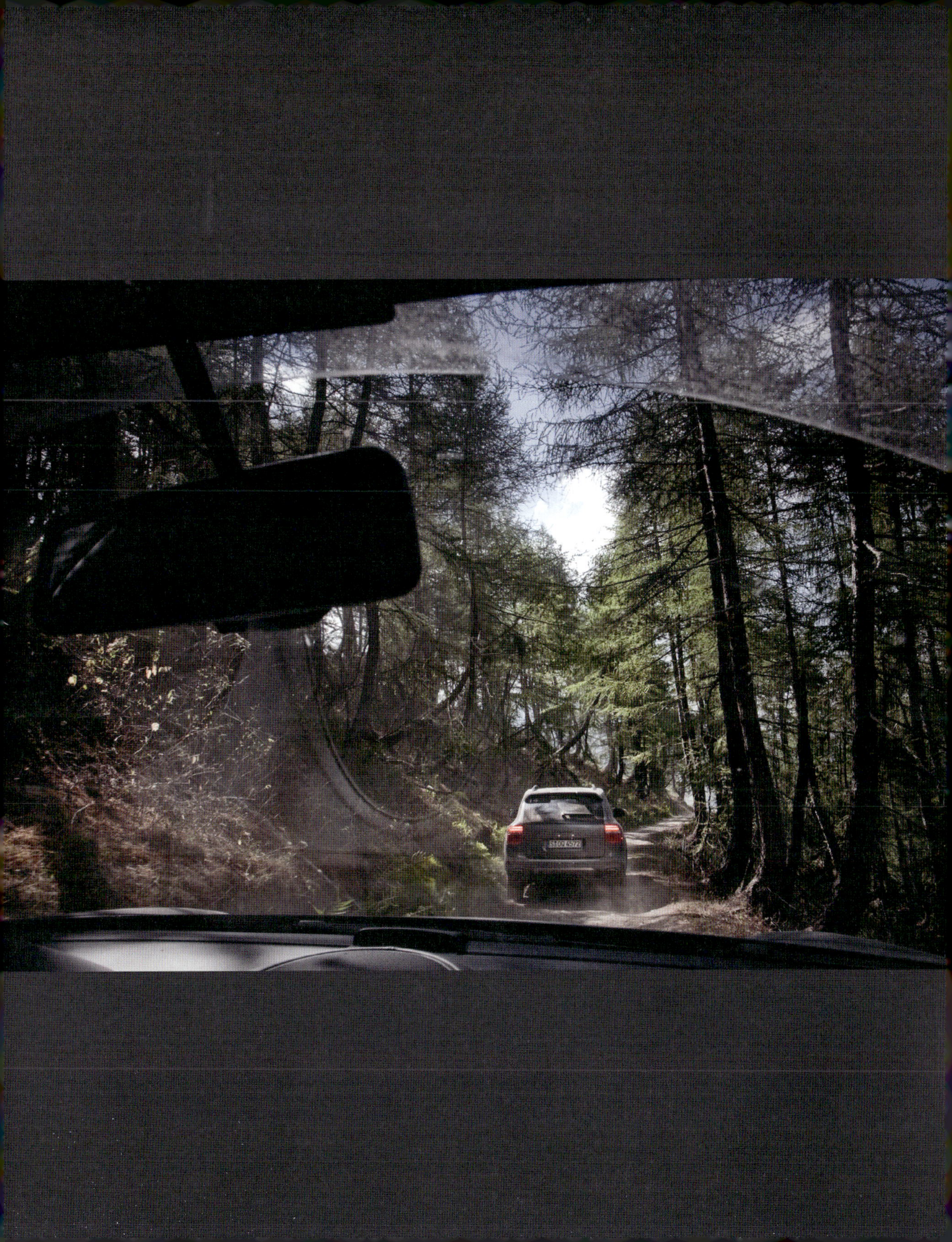

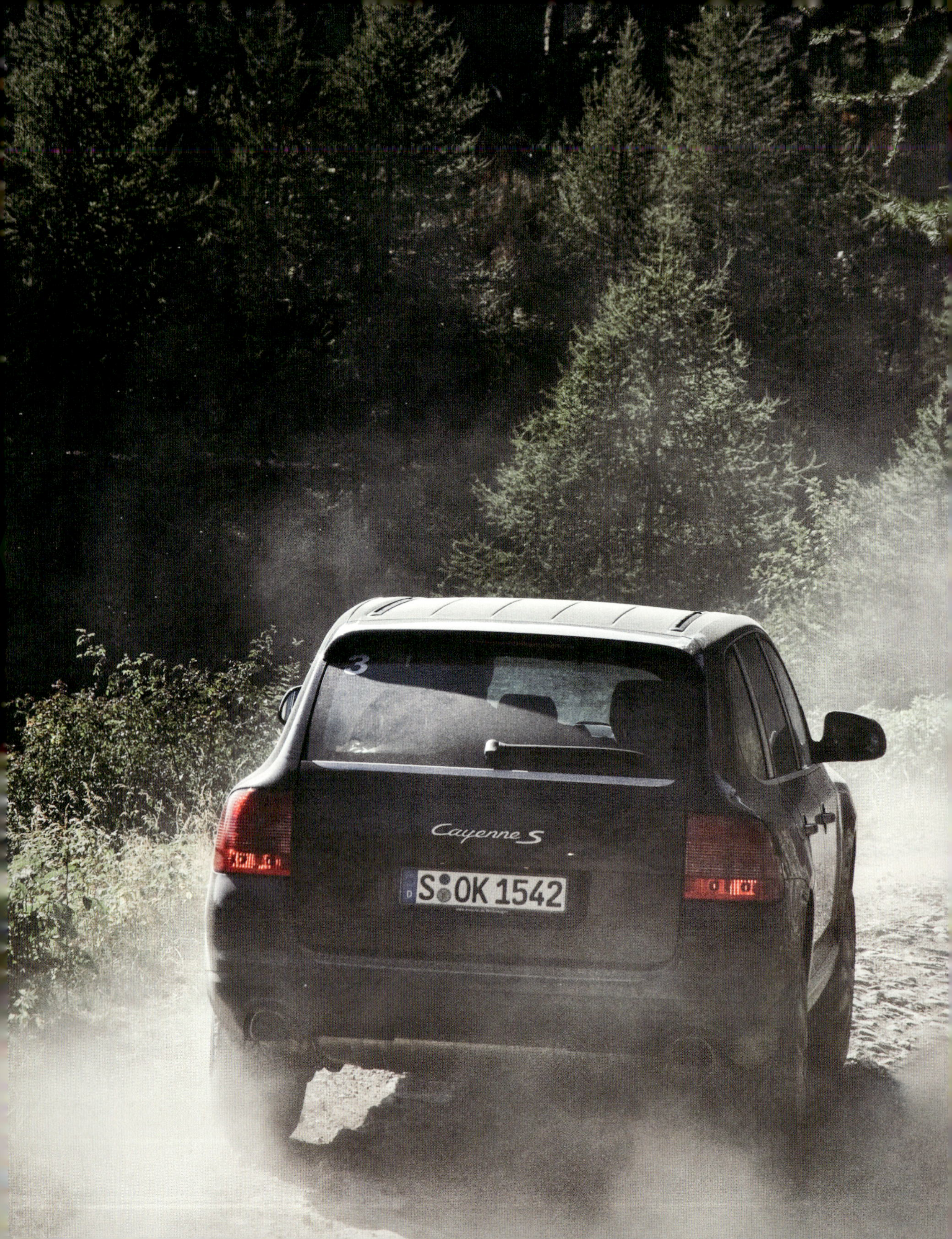
3
Cayenne S
S OK 1542

Fly Away

Fly, day, fly
away from this
dark time,
above these
sombre dreams,
fly, o fly away…

Fly, day, fly
into that
deep night,
towards
a better morrow,
fly, o fly on…

Fly, day, fly,
beyond these
dull times,
out of these
dim rooms,
fly off to eternity…

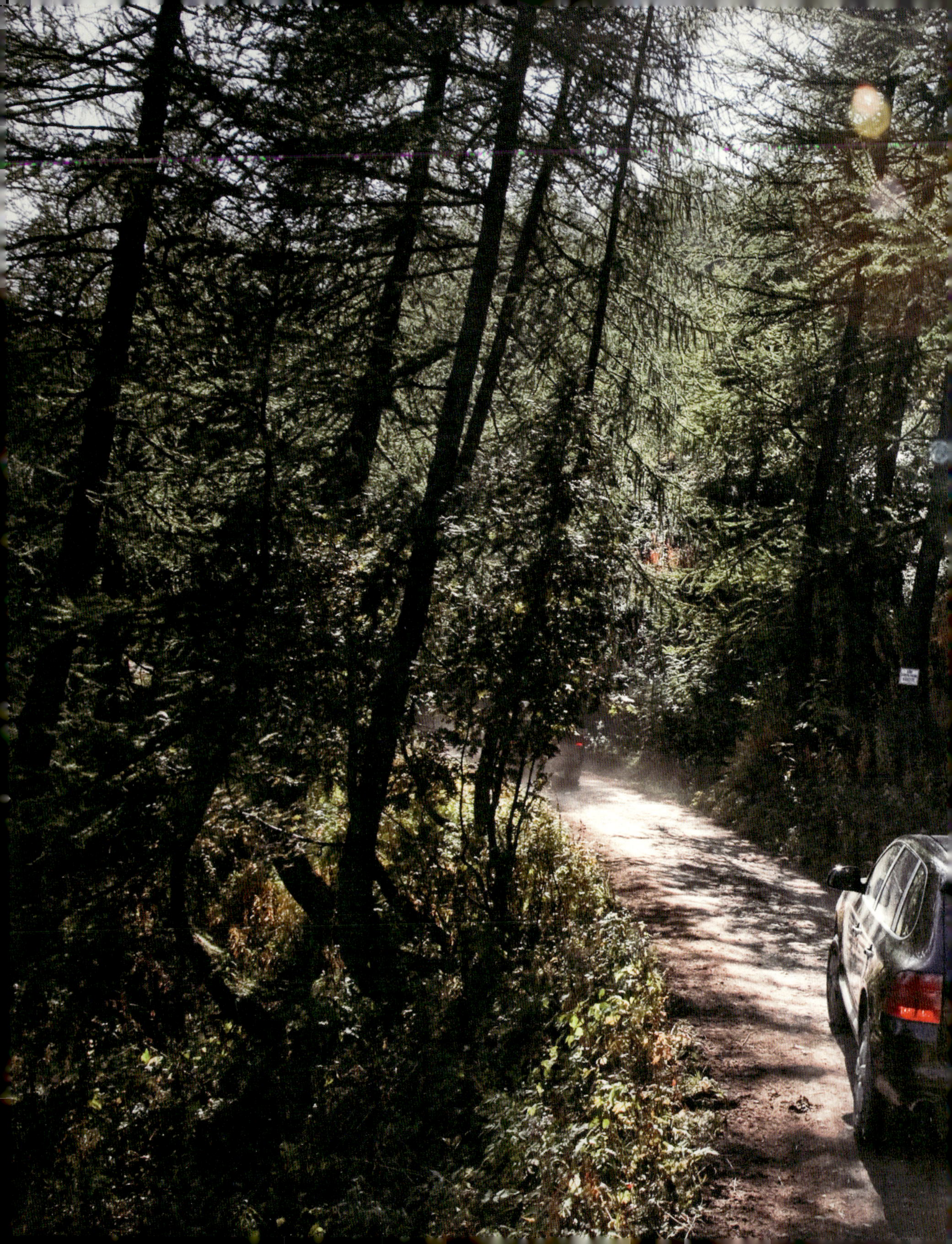

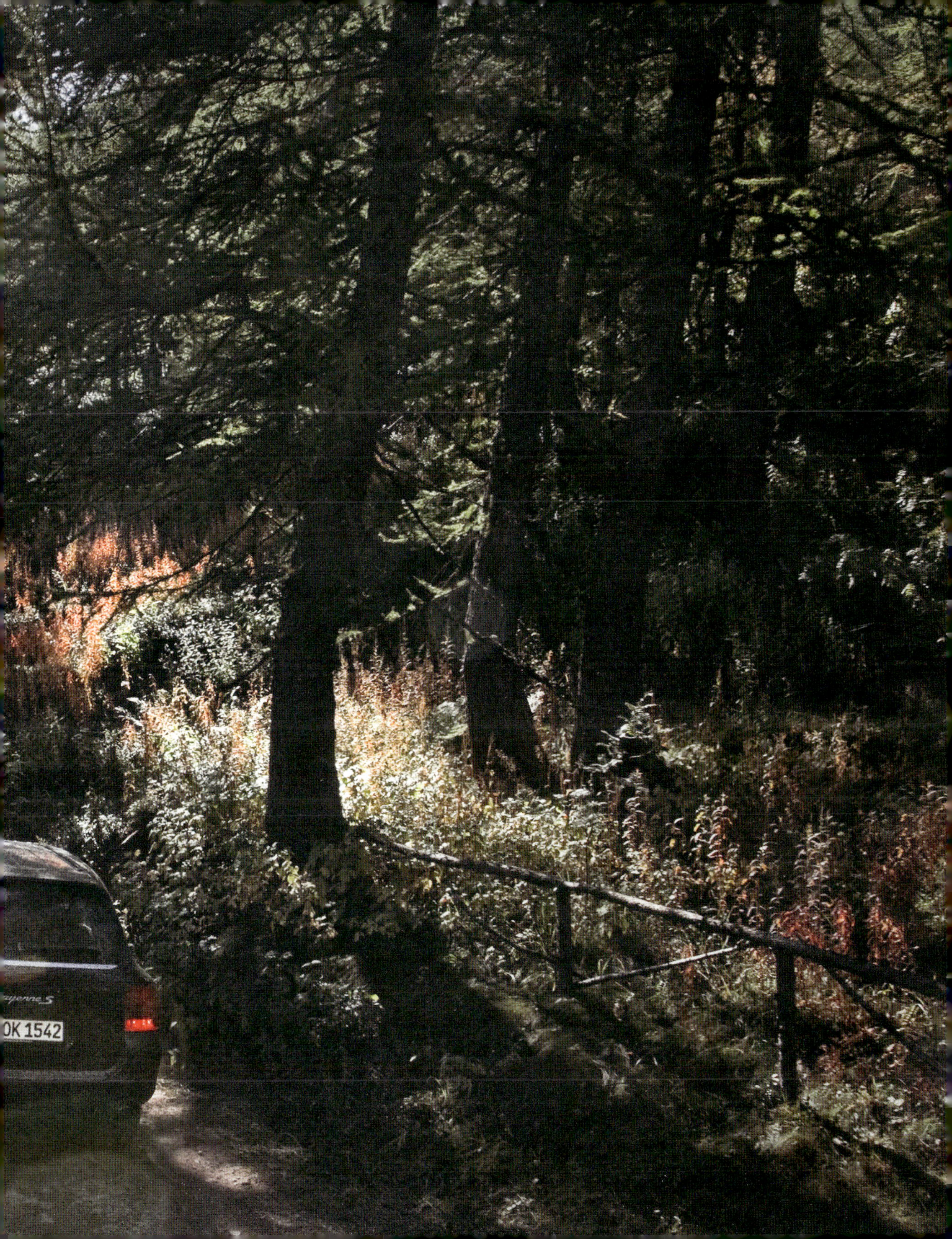
OK 1542

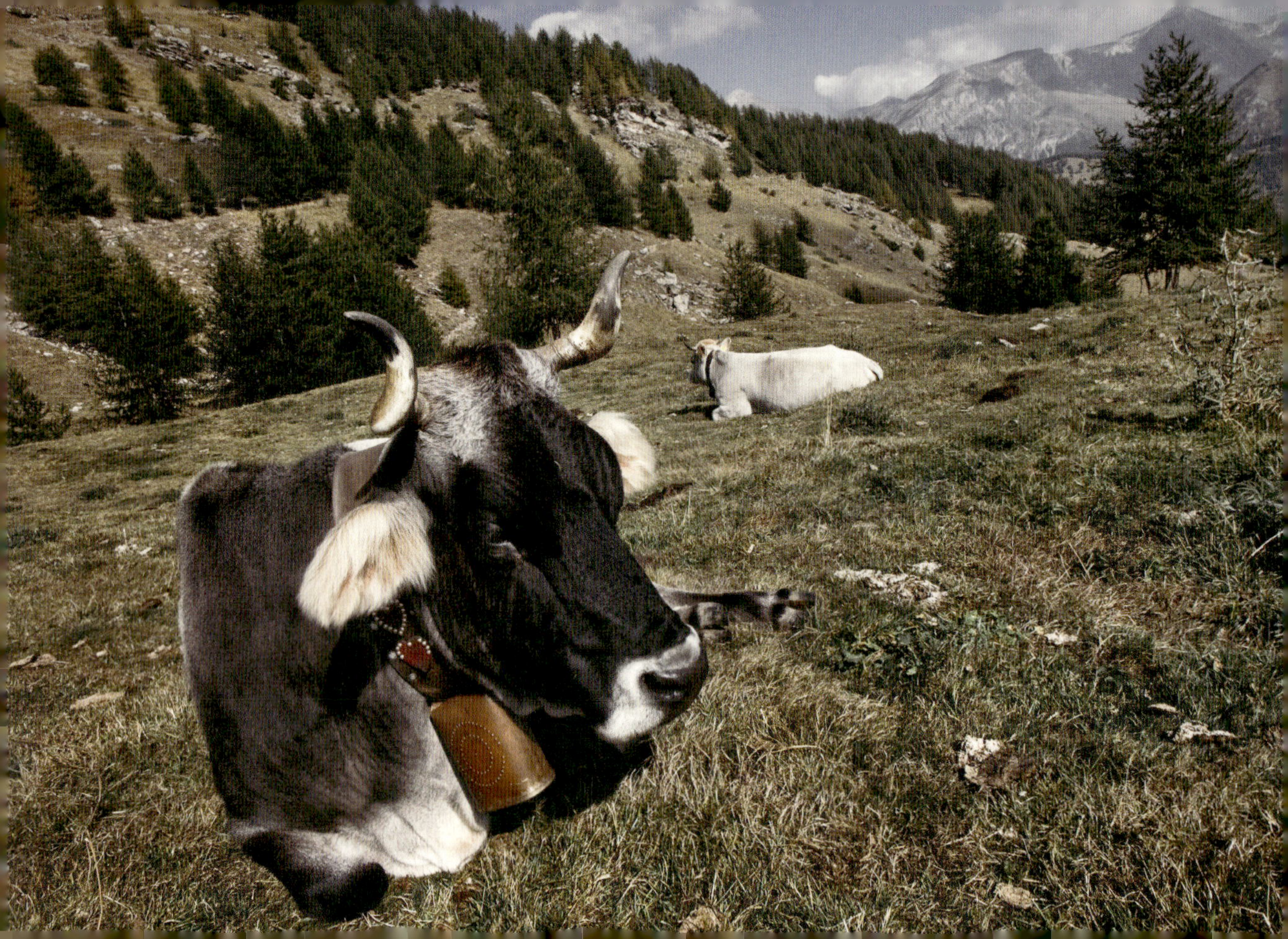

Calm Within

All is calm
I am calm
I have calmness within
I am full of calm
I am calmness itself
Calm

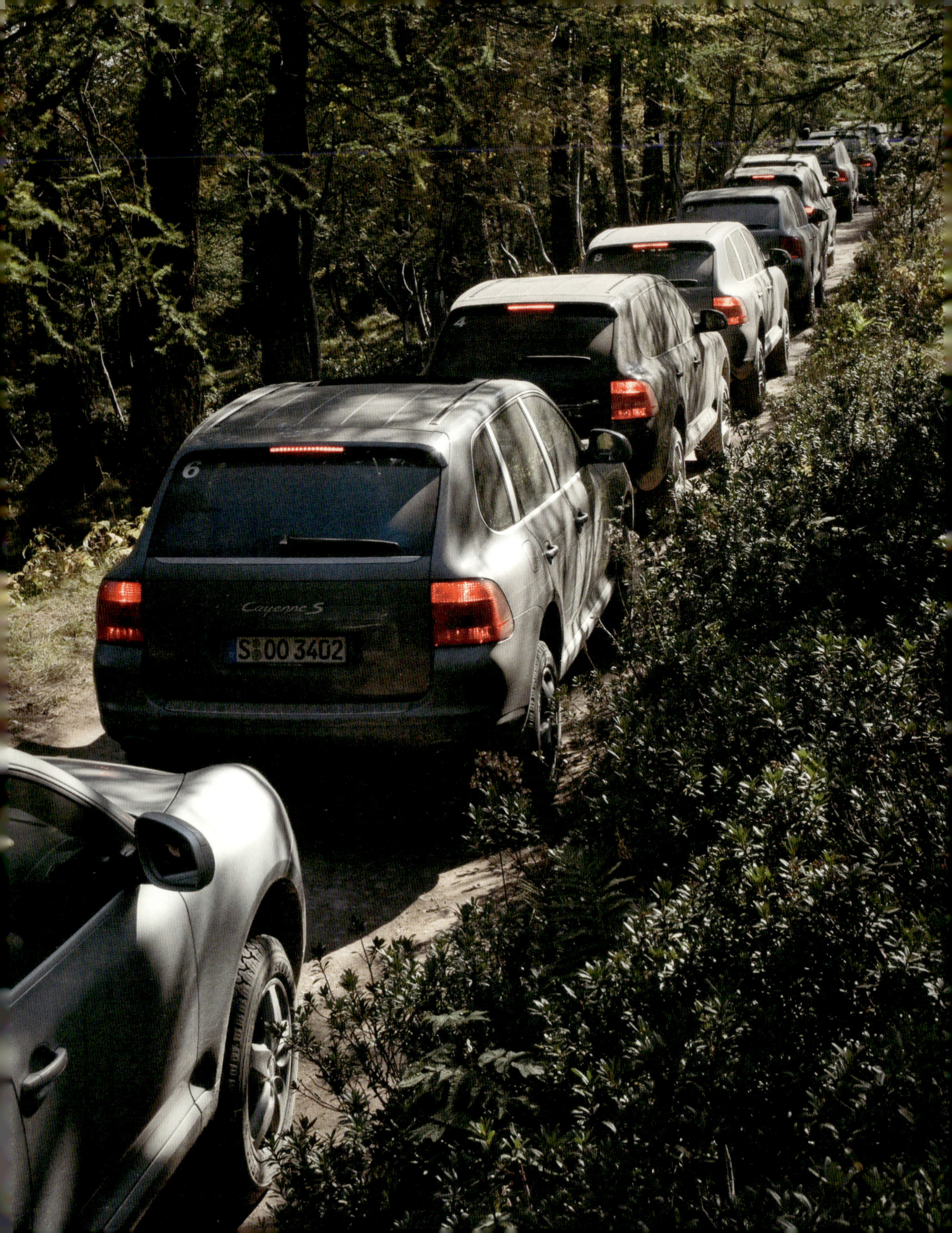
6
Cayenne S
S 00 3402

Devotion

The meadows now are laid to rest
And summer's time gives way to frost,
That all with Nature's breath infused
May quietly be with new life blessed.

The moon shines on in time and space
And wondrously the stars unfold
High up in their own heavenly place,
Their lofty mysteries untold.

And so we are drawn on gently
To the night that is most profound,
When winter's depth most ardently
Rings and sings to the Christmas sound.

The Beacon

Dashing against the rocks, the waves
Leap from the vast unruly sea,
And soaring above the steep cliff-face
Seagulls swirl and mewl about me.

The velvet meadow is tranquil and sweet
And soft the sheep benignly graze,
While wild ponies canter beyond the trees
Around this peaceful, secluded place.

Up on the rocky promontory
Enthroned on those majestic heights,
The beacon lords it over the sea
Standing firm as ever on stormy nights.

Now the beacon basks in the sun's warm rays
But behind that bland exterior
Many a story untold remains
About the reefs of that rugged shore.

Dispersed along the nearby strands
Scattered, rusting, iron rails
Tell a tale of striving human hands,
Contending with wild seas and gales.

How many seamen stalwart and brave
Must have struggled with their fate in vain,
Found off that shore a watery grave,
For none of them came back again.

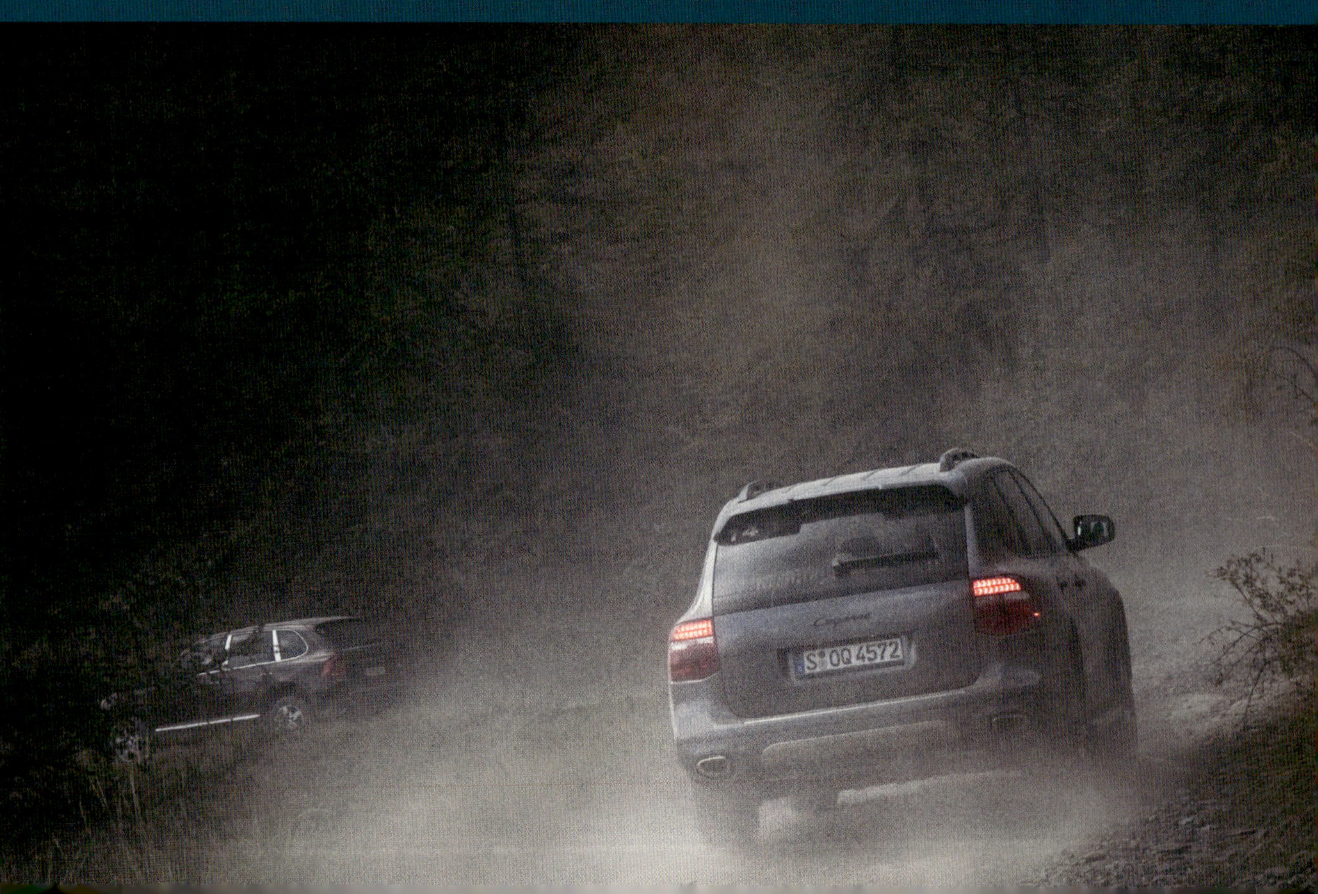

Wives and children waiting at home,
Between prayer and hope have spent their years
Full of foreboding, always alone,
Dreading the answer to their worst fears.

And as men grow older with each year
Just as sure as the flowers of spring,
On the mighty rocks that we see from here
Ships are still getting wrecked and sink.

That beacon towers on silently
Pondering the deep abyss,
While below the black coils of sea
Wind in serpentine turns and twists.

Should ever the beacon's masonry
Tumble and fall into the sea,
And with it the sailors sad history,
That place would still a wasteland be.

Waves against cliffs battle ever on
And all things on earth will die as decreed –
But there is a never-ending song
That tells us the spirit will be freed.

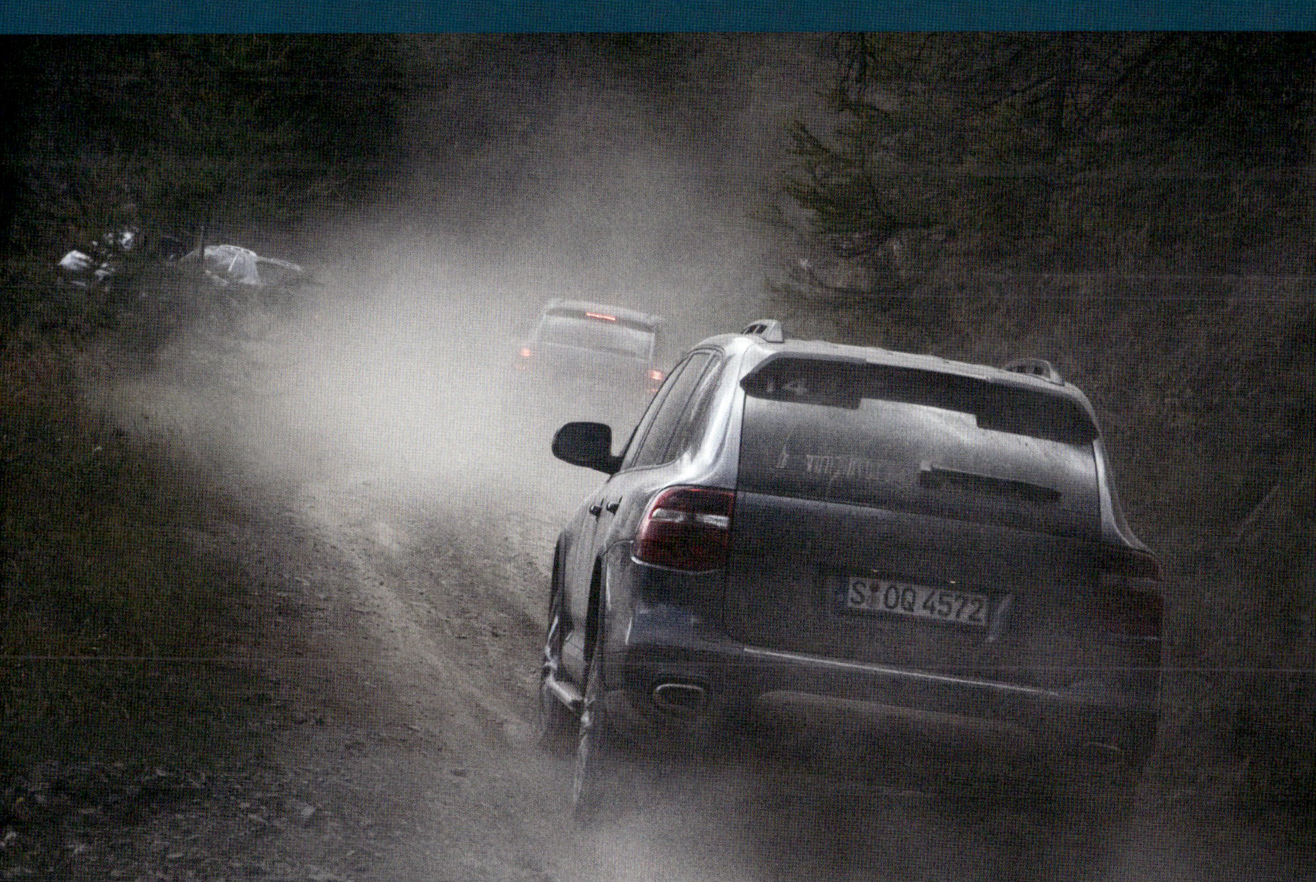

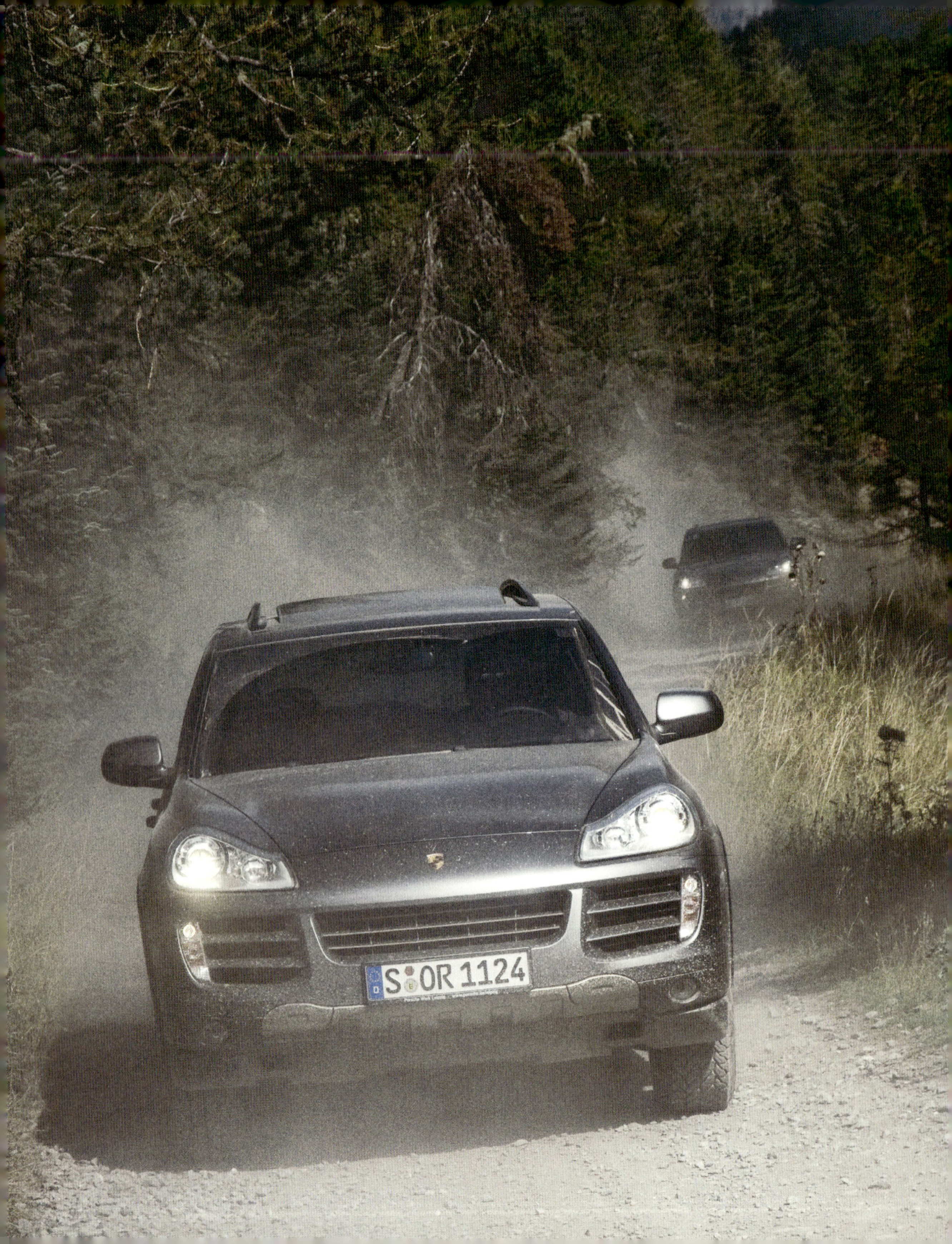
S OR 1124

Storm

The trees toss and stir
The airs vibrate
The leaves quiver
Dreams agitate.

The storm-clouds dash
The stars are alight
The rain-drops lash
Hailstones ignite.

The lightening sparks
The thunder breaks
Thoughts spin and dart
My purpose awakes.

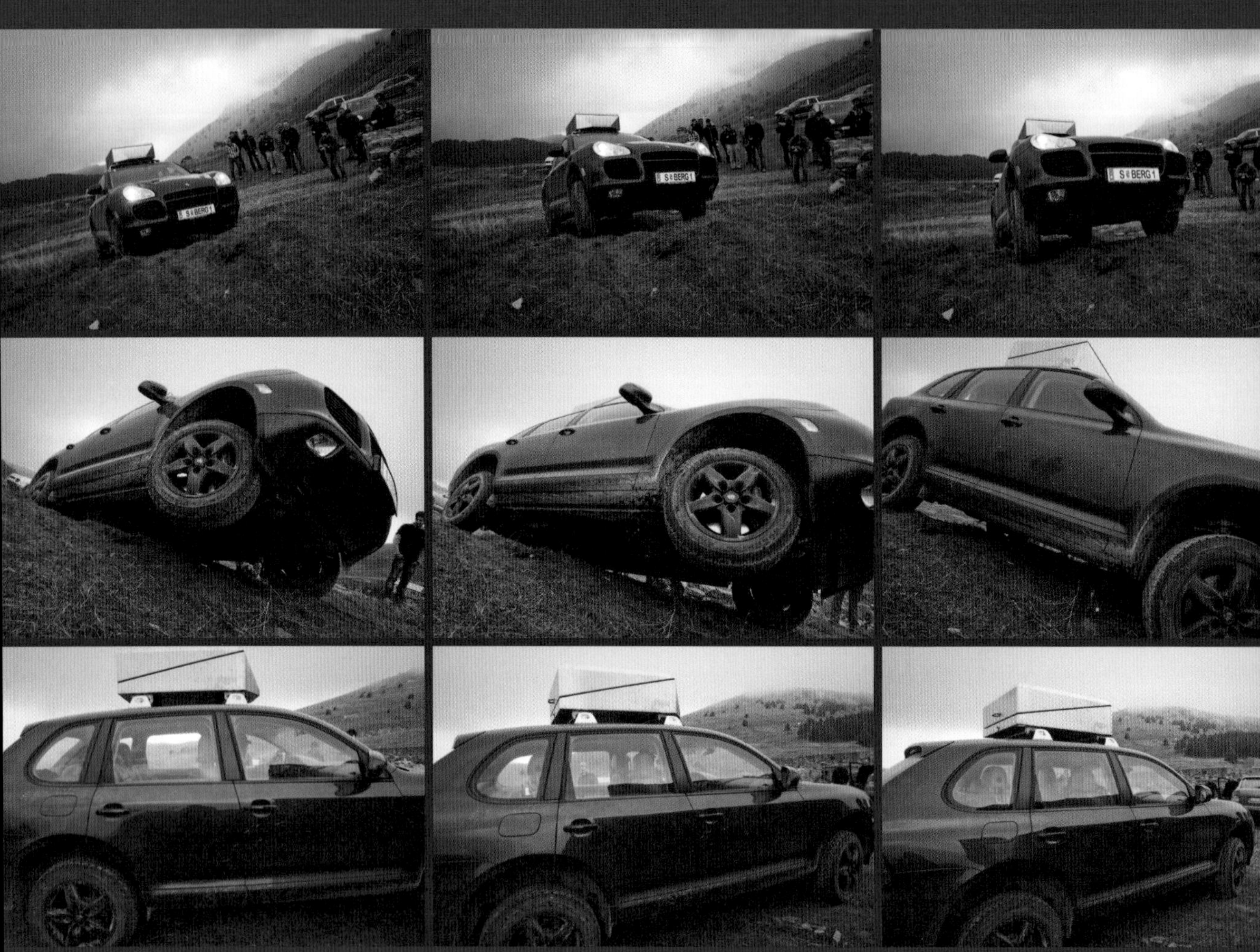

New energy is born
when hurdles are overcome.

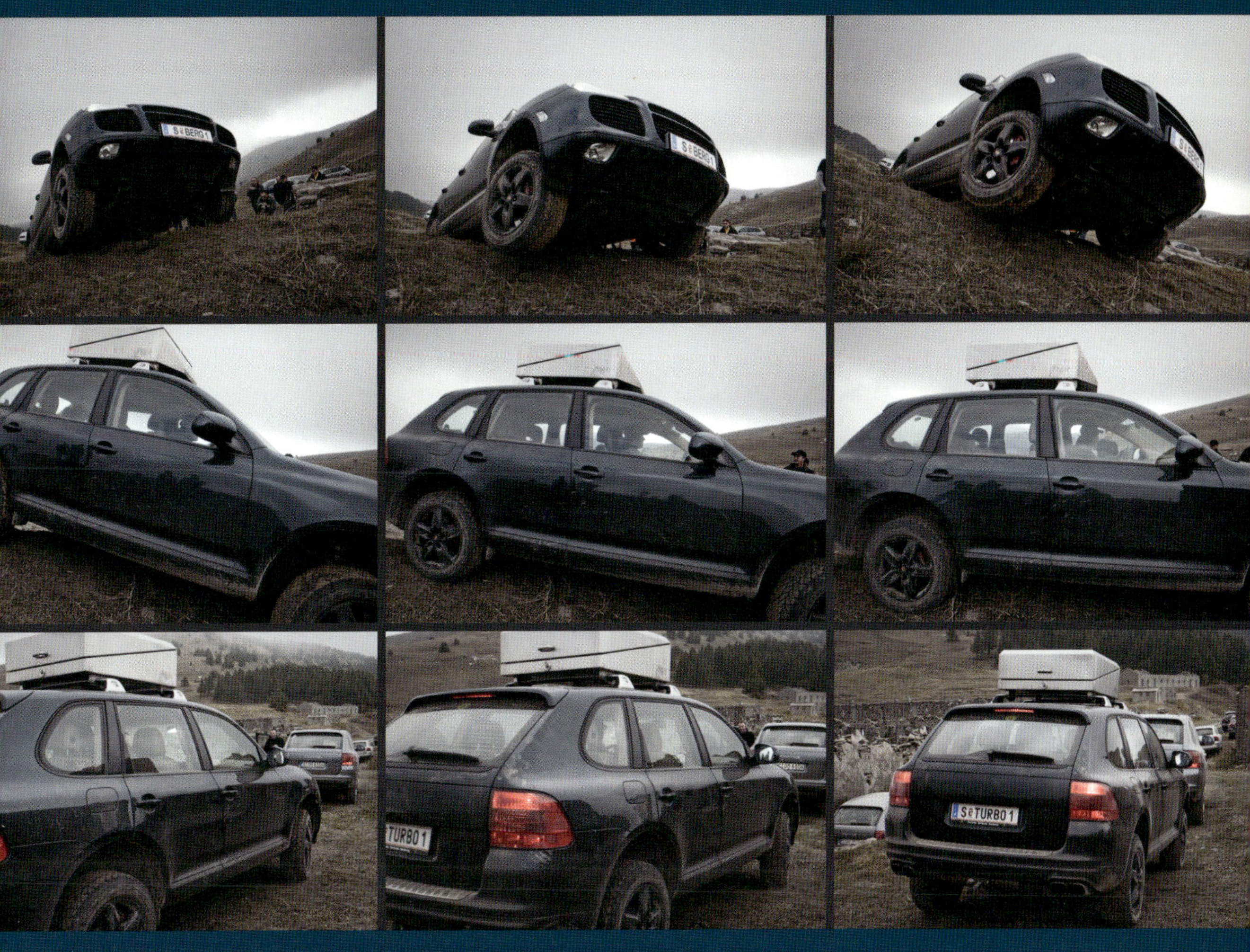

It is often only the stony road
that leads to the special situation in life.

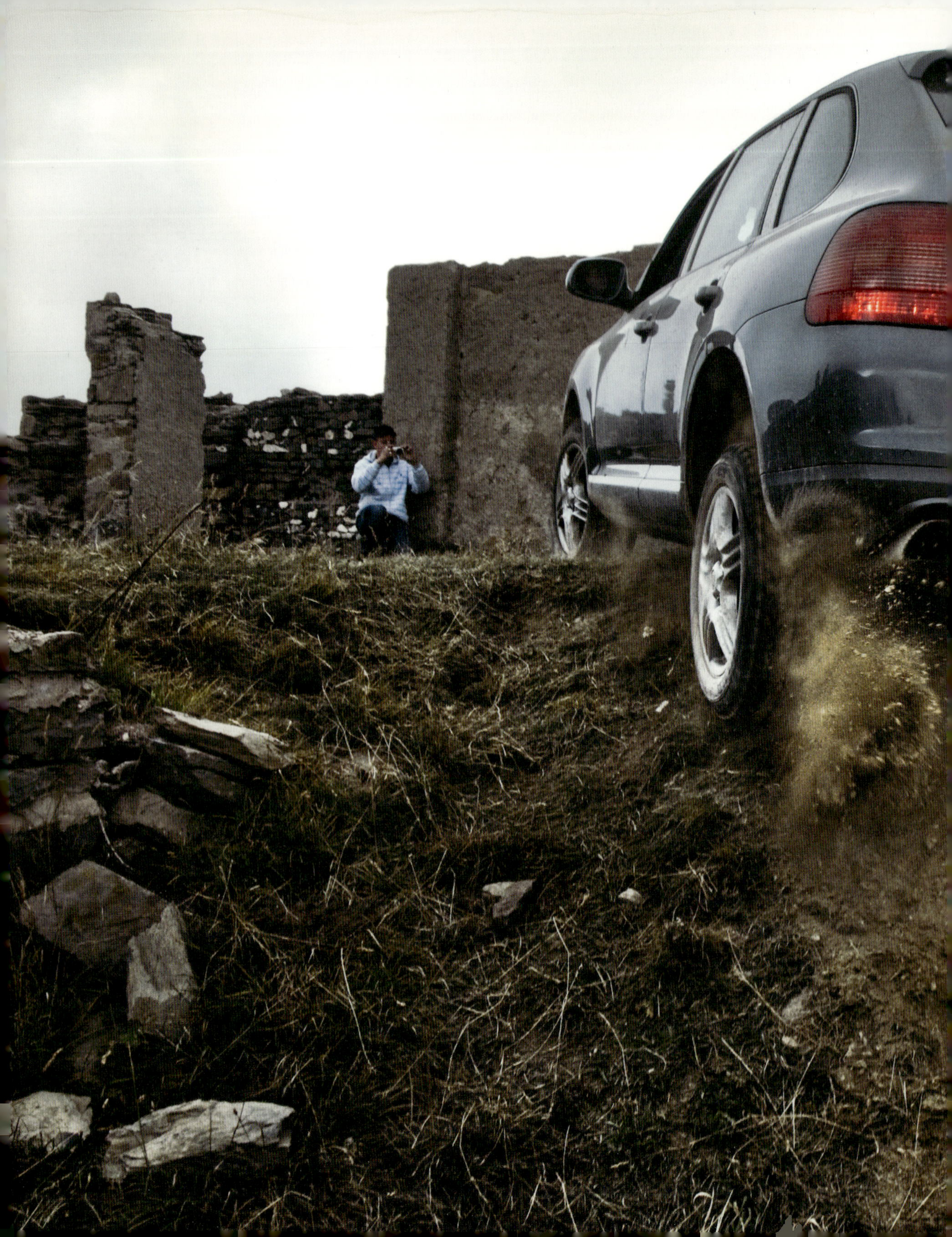

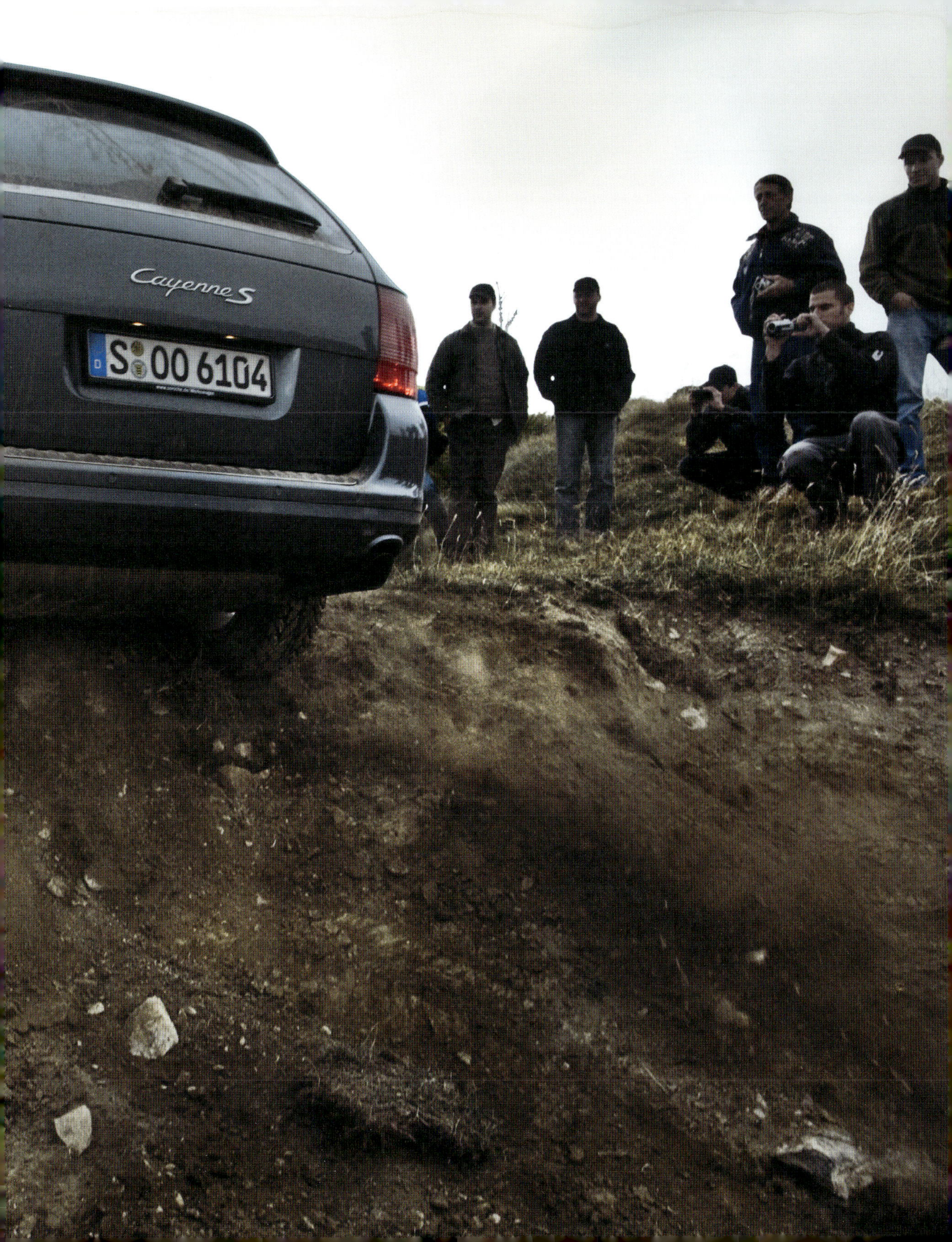
Cayenne S
S 00 6104

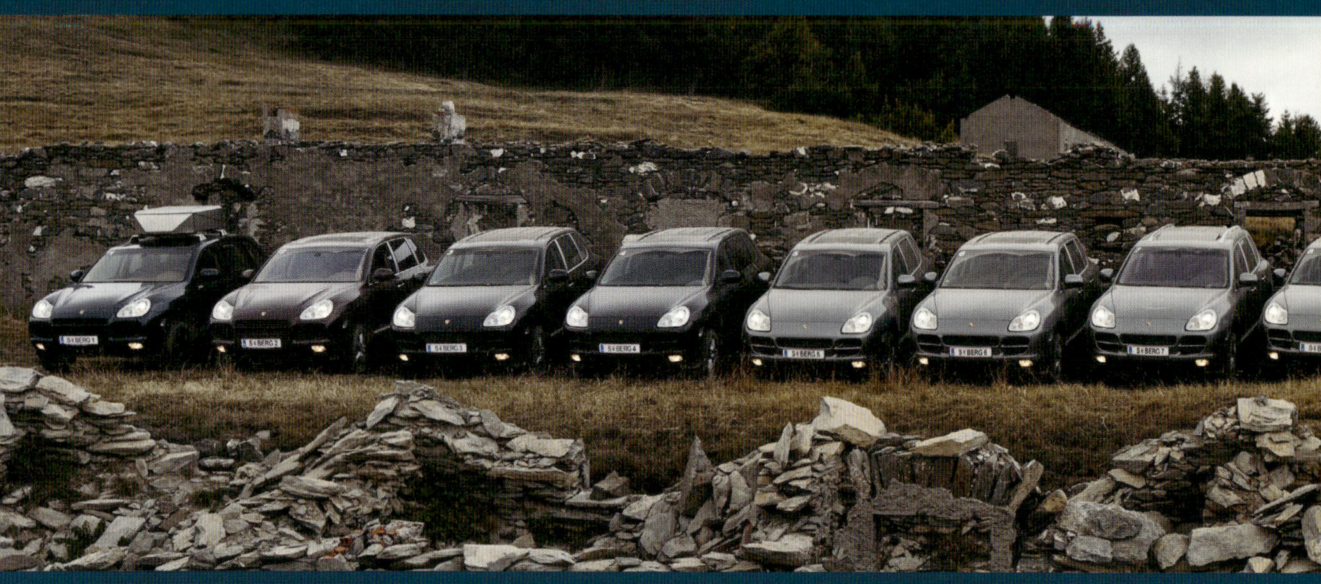

A Sunset On The Sea

On the horizon
A ball of fire
Is sinking slow
Unto the wide sea –

And clouds are dreaming
In the evening glow
Of the coming day –

In a glory of hues
Their cheeks aflame
To distant reflections
They sultry give way –

As o'er silvery sands
Surge silently
Incandescent waves –

And choirs of crests
In a fervent hush
Press for the shore –

So down it slipped
Noiselessly
The last of day's light
To the shiny sea –

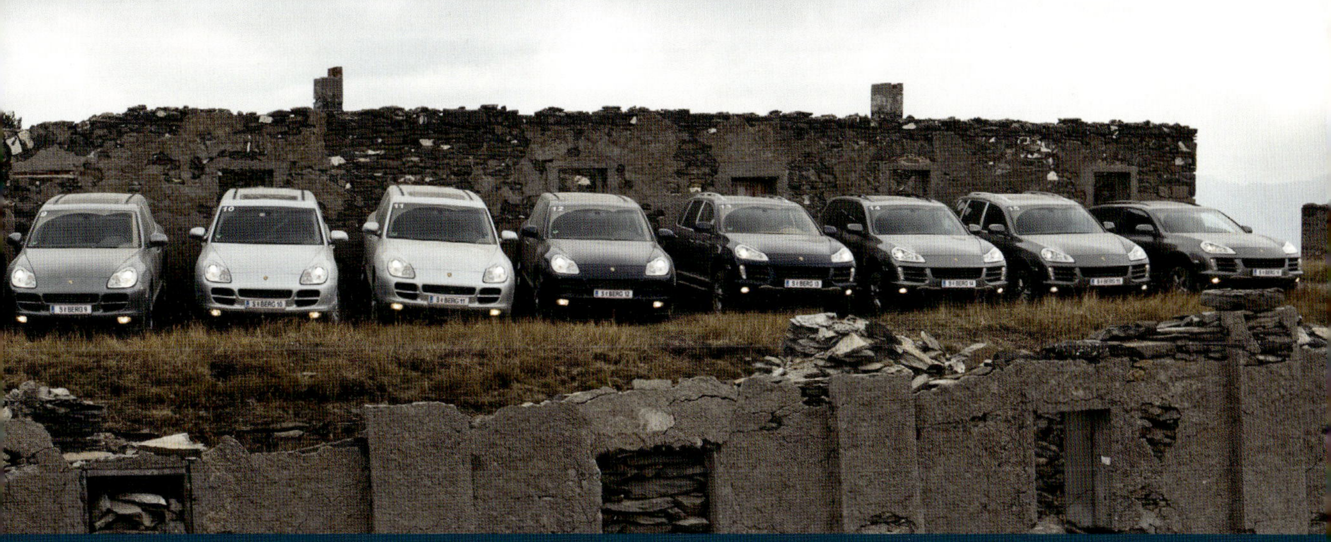

The red sky billowed out
To imbibe the last gleam
As peaceful dark rose
About this night –

The dream of the clouds
Is ever dedicated
To night's illumination
While the heaven unveils
Deep intimations
Of his nature to man
And sonorous hails
Now the dark –

That sound of eternity
Colour-faded – but hark –
No rain falls nor is heard
Any whisper so faint –

Tho' the day lives on
In memory
That is soon flown
To the maze of stars…

I love you
fair sunset!

I revere you
lofty starlight!

I reach out
to you
great universe…night!

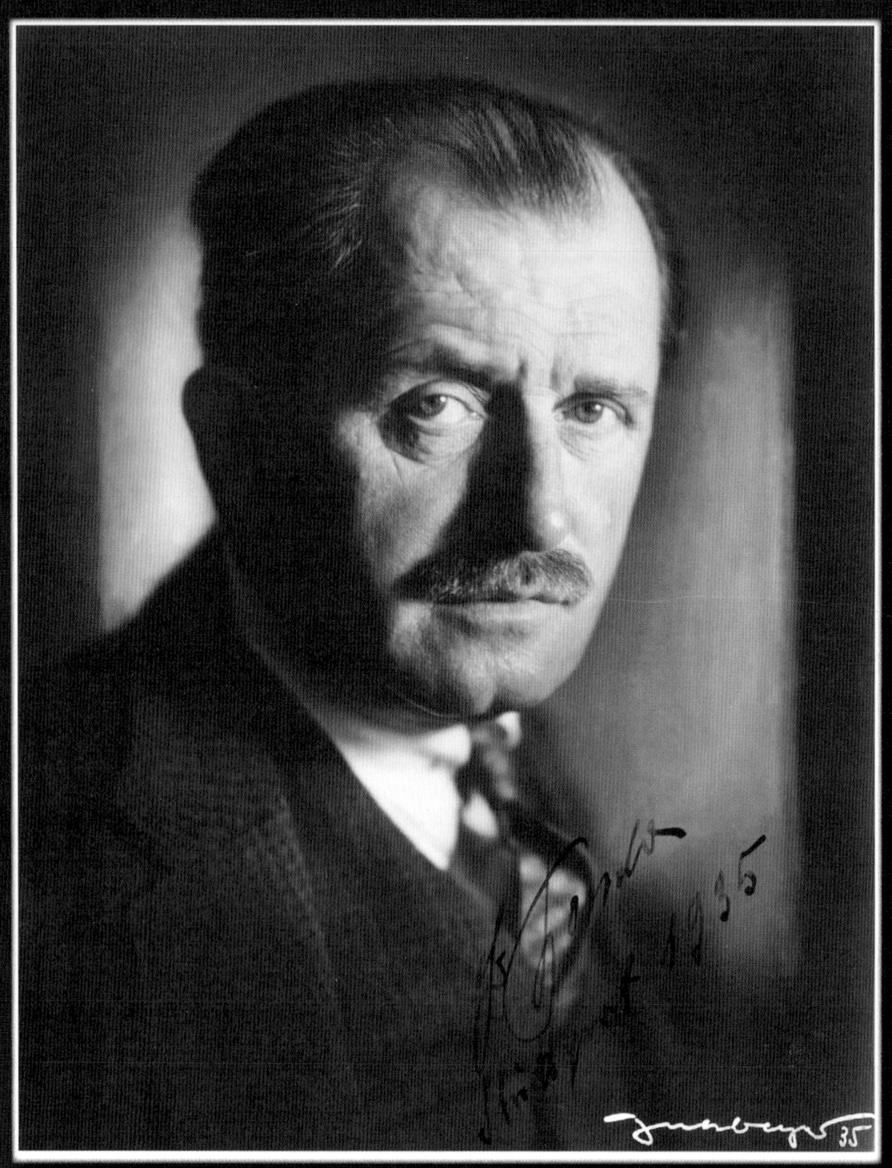

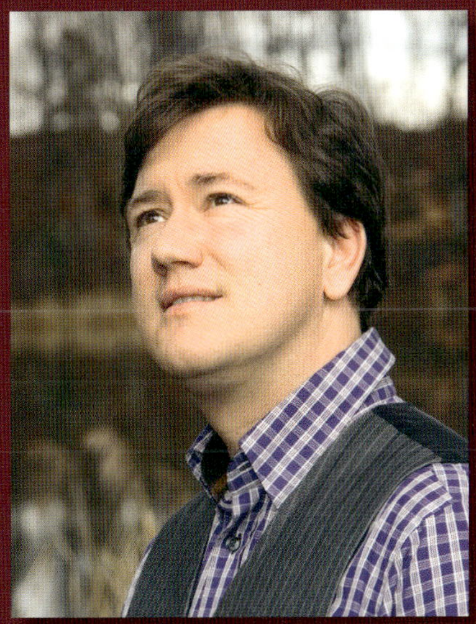

This work was your construction from the start
Here vision, vigour and values played a role
A valiant spirit of invention was your part
Nothing could deflect you from your goal
Keenly you strove to build for posterity –

Your able hands and cool head made your art
Oblivious of hatred, doubt or envy –
Until forever, thank-you from my heart!

Yours, Peter Daniell

Previous publications of Peter Daniell Porsche

(available in German only)

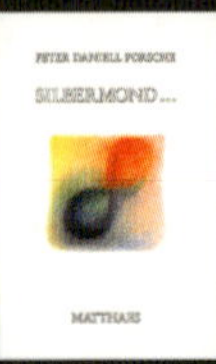

Silver Moon...
A collection of first and early poems taking its tenor from the four temperaments into which it is subdivided.
Stitch-bound book, hardcover, with partially coloured cover.
104 pages, DIN A6, portrait.

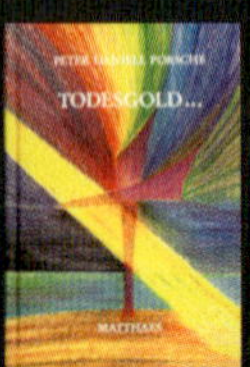

Death's Gold...
A collection of personal poems on the subject of death, the transitory nature of things, resurrection and reincarnation.
Stitch-bound book, hardcover, with full-colour cover.
104 pages, DIN A6, portrait.

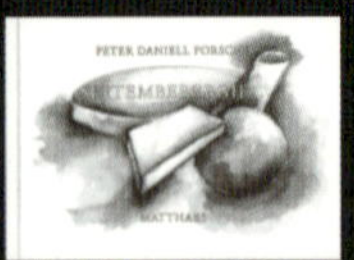

September Orgy...
A collection of epigrams composed one September in the course of a few days. The contents refer not only to profound human questions but also to ordinary basic principles of life on this earth of ours.
Stitch-bound book, hardcover, with duotone cover.
104 pages, large print, DIN A6, landscape.

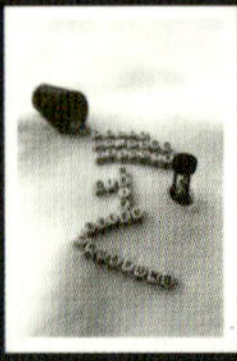

Mature High-School Graduation Exams
An attempt to come to terms with present-day school-leaving problems from personal experience and the point of view that this tends to be a question of performance and not true ability.
Stitch-bound book, softcover, with duotone cover.
104 pages, DIN A6, portrait.

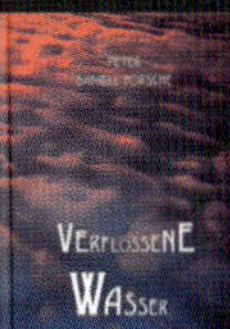

Water under the Bridge

A collection of over forty poems from a protracted gestation period for lonely, timeless and hopeful hours of the past, present and the future.
Stitch-bound book, hardcover, with full-colour cover.
104 pages, DIN A6, portrait.

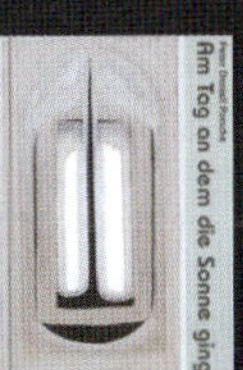

The Day the Sun Went Out

A story in novel form: a hard-back book with blank pages is the birthday present from an aunt to her nephew who has just turned fourteen… The day after his birthday he decides to write a diary of his own. Although he has never given much thought to his past, it is always threatening to catch up with him, so he starts scribbling away as fast as he can…
Stitch-bound book, hardcover, with full-colour cover.
104 pages, DIN A6, portrait.

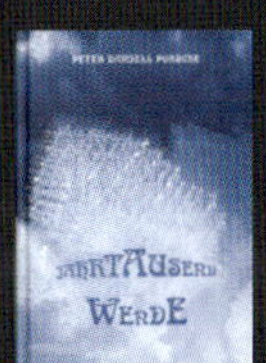

The Millennium

Poems to mark the turn of the millennium: searching questions, visionary thoughts about the future and romantic images from the years gone by as well as of present and emerging expectations. Along these lines an attempt is made at a modern though not arbitrarily abstract expression of thoughts partly in rhyme, partly simply carried along by the language.
Stitch-bound book, hardcover, with full-colour cover.
104 pages, DIN A6, portrait.

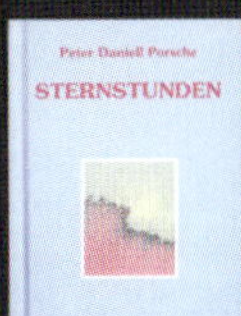

Turning Points

A collection of sayings for children before birth and after – up to school age.
Stitch-bound book, hardcover, with full-colour cover.
104 pages, DIN A6, portrait.

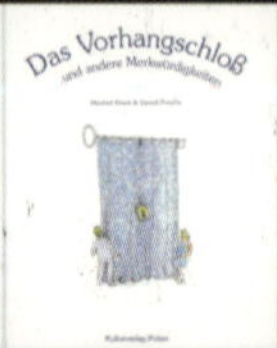

The Padlock

A collection of humorous poems. These poems aim at providing readers with a chance to step back from the hustle and bustle of daily life and, in getting in touch with their own inner clown, rediscover the pleasures of peace and quiet with humour and perhaps some reflection too.
Stitch-bound book, hardcover, with full-colour cover. More than 60 coloured illustrations as well as 57 accompanying poems.
144 pages, oversized DIN A5, portrait.

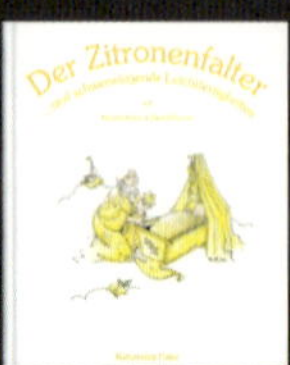

The Brimestone Butterfly

A collection of humorous poems with matching colourful illustrations. These poems with their lighthearted but meditative touch illuminate the diversity of possible word associations in the German language. Day-to-day life is lifted up as on the wings of the butterfly, out of the humdrum, but at the same time one's thoughts are drawn down to earth to fathom all the more keenly, the nature of life's responsibilities.
Stitch-bound book, hardcover, with full-colour cover.
144 pages, oversized DIN A5, portrait.

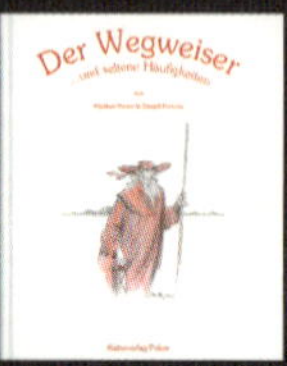

The Guide

The last book of this humorous poem trilogy rounds off the cycle that started with the childlike, light touch of The Padlock, continued with The Brimestone Butterfly alighting on the earth and now concludes with the leaving of this earth. The Guide's forty-four poems are more serious than those of the earlier books but then this is addressed in the first place to adults rather than to children, as was the case in its predecessors.
Stitch-bound book, hardcover, with full-colour cover.
167 pages, DIN A6, portrait.

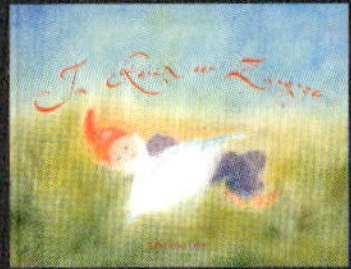

In the Realm of the Gnomes

Peter Daniell Porsche's first children's book contains 14 poems in which an attempt is made to describe the atmosphere of the realm of the gnomes in a variety of ways. Water-colours and chalk sketches done by the author's mother, Kuni Porsche, subtly encourage the listening child to follow its own fantasy deeper into this world. The texts are hand-written by Elizabeth Presch.
Stitch-bound book, hardcover, with full-colour cover.
30 pages, oversized DIN A4, landscape.

Proceeds from the twelve books listed here are donated to the Paracelsus School Salzburg (educational institute for children and young people lacking social and emotional skills).
For sales, please contact us at:
www.einporschegehtaufreisen.at
www.polzer.net
www.kunstschrift.at
www.kulturzentrum-stjakob.at

We take care in every way to ensure your best possible satisfaction.